Beginning AngularJS

Andrew Grant

Apress®

Beginning AngularJS

ISBN-13 (pbk): 978-1-4842-0161-9

ISBN-13 (electronic): 978-1-4842-0160-2

Managing Director: Welmoed Spahr
Lead Editor: Louise Corrigan
Developmental Editor: Gary Schwartz
Technical Reviewer: Andrew Markham-Davies
Editorial Board: Steve Anglin, Mark Beckner, Ewan Buckingham, Gary Cornell, Louise Corrigan,
    Jim DeWolf, Jonathan Gennick, Robert Hutchinson, Michelle Lowman, James Markham, Matthew Moodie,
    Jeff Olson, Jeffrey Pepper, Douglas Pundick, Ben Renow-Clarke, Dominic Shakeshaft, Gwenan Spearing,
    Matt Wade, Steve Weiss
Coordinating Editor: Christine Ricketts
Copy Editor: Michael Laraque
Compositor: SPi Global
Indexer: SPi Global
Artist: SPi Global
Cover Designer: Anna Ishchenko

Distributed to the book trade worldwide by Springer Science+Business Media New York, 233 Spring Street, 6th Floor, New York, NY 10013. Phone 1-800-SPRINGER, fax (201) 348-4505, e-mail orders-ny@springer-sbm.com, or visit www.springeronline.com. Apress Media, LLC is a California LLC and the sole member (owner) is Springer Science + Business Media Finance Inc (SSBM Finance Inc). SSBM Finance Inc is a Delaware corporation.

For information on translations, please e-mail rights@apress.com, or visit www.apress.com.

Apress and friends of ED books may be purchased in bulk for academic, corporate, or promotional use. eBook versions and licenses are also available for most titles. For more information, reference our Special Bulk Sales–eBook Licensing web page at www.apress.com/bulk-sales.

Any source code or other supplementary material referenced by the author in this text is available to readers at www.apress.com. For detailed information about how to locate your book's source code, go to www.apress.com/source-code/.

I would like to dedicate this book to my wonderful wife, Monica, and my amazing children, Jennifer, Catie and Christopher.

Contents at a Glance

Contents

About the Author

Andrew Grant has been developing websites for fun and profit for over 18 years. He is currently a full-time Web Developer with a passion for technology and life on the cutting edge. Andrew holds various web development related vendor certifications and an Advanced Diploma in Software Development. He can be reached via his personal web page at http://andrewgrant.net.au.

About the Technical Reviewer

Andrew Markham-Davies is a software engineer from Yorkshire, England who has worked on software for the like of Sky, BBC, ADT and DePuy Synthes. While he's has worked extensively with C#, java and php in the past, his passion is Javascript and front end development. A big fan of mv* style frameworks, Andrew found AngularJS the perfect tool for building rich, well structured javascript heavy applications.

He is a keen advocate of refactoring and applying engineering principals to Javascript including automation, tooling and testing best practices.

Andrew can be found on twitter at `http://twitter.com/atmd83` and blogs at `http://atmd.co.uk`.

Acknowledgments

I would like to thank my wonderful wife, Monica, for helping me write this book and do my day job at the same time. I would also like to thank the amazing Apress editorial team, in particular my technical reviewer, Andrew Markham-Davies, for his valuable feedback.

CHAPTER 1

JavaScript You Need to Know

If you want to learn AngularJS, then you will need to know JavaScript. However, you don't have to be a JavaScript expert. If you already know JavaScript fairly well, you can skip this chapter and use it as a handy reference, although I will refer you back to here at certain points in the book.

■ **Note**   It isn't uncommon to hear people refer to the AngularJS framework as simply *Angular*. As *Beginning AngularJS* is the title of this book, I will refer to it as *AngularJS* throughout.

There is only enough space in this book to cover the basics very briefly; although I will expand and reinforce certain topics in relevant chapters as the book progresses.

JavaScript Primer

When compared to many other programming languages, such as C++ and Java, JavaScript is relatively easy to pick up and use, and in the following sections, I will get you started by explaining how to include scripts on your web page; how to use various control structures, statements, functions, and objects; and I will address a few other topics, such as callbacks and JSON.

Including Scripts on a Page

This is where it all begins: we need some way to tell the web browser that it has to process our JavaScript. To do this, we use the `script` tag. Listing 1-1 uses the `src` attribute to point to the location of a JavaScript file.

Listing 1-1. Referencing an External Script

```
<!DOCTYPE html>
<html>
  <head>
    <title>JavaScript Primer</title>
  </head>
  <body>
    <!-- reference the myScript.js script file -->
    <script src="scripts/myScript.js"></script>

  </body>
</html>
```

In this case, the file is called myScript.js, and it resides in a directory named scripts. You can also write your script directly in the HTML file itself. Listing 1-2 demonstrates this technique.

Listing 1-2. Using an Inline Script

```
<!DOCTYPE html>
    <html>
    <head>
    <title>JavaScript Primer</title>
    </head>
    <body>

    <!-- an inline script -->
    <script>console.log("Hello");</script>

    </body>
</html>
```

Most of the time, it is better to use the first approach and reference a separate file containing your scripts. This way, you can reuse the same scripts in multiple files. The second method, usually referred to as an inline script, is most often used when reuse isn't a requirement, or simply for convenience.

Assuming that the file script.js contains the exact same code as the inline script, the browser output would be as follows:

```
Hello
```

For the most part, I will include complete code listings in this chapter, so that you can load them into your browser and experiment. You will learn a lot more by tinkering with code and viewing its output than by relying solely on this drive-by introduction.

Statements

A *JavaScript application* is essentially a collection of expressions and statements. Without the aid of other constructs, such as branching and looping statements, which I will discuss shortly, these are executed by the browser, one after the other. Each usually exists on its own line and, optionally, ends with a semicolon (see Listing 1-3).

Listing 1-3. Statement Execution

```
<!DOCTYPE html>
<html>
<head >
    <title>JavaScript Primer</title>
    <script>
        console.log("I am a statement");
        console.log("I am also a statement");
    </script>
</head>
```

```
<body>
<script>
    console.log("Here is another statement");
    console.log("Here is the last statement");
</script>
</body>
</html>
```

The preceding listing simply logs output to the console and produces the results shown in the output below. If you are unfamiliar with the location of the browser's JavaScript console, you can access it on Chrome, using Tools ➤ JavaScript Console or, if you use Internet Explorer, by pressing F12 to bring up the Developer Tools and then clicking the console icon. Of course, you can use your favorite search engine to find out where the JavaScript console is hiding in your preferred browser. I will be using the handy console.log() approach quite extensively in this chapter, to display the program output.

I hope the output shown below is as you would expect it to appear. Although I use two separate script tags here, the output would have been the same even if I had put all of the statements into the first script tag in the exact same order. The browser doesn't really care; it just deals with the scripts as it finds them.

```
I am a statement
I am also a statement
Here is another statement
Here is the last statement
```

You may have picked up on my comment earlier about semicolons being optional. This fact is often a source of confusion. The easiest way to avoid any confusion or code mistakes is simply to use semicolons as though they are required. Don't give yourself the option of omitting them. Nonetheless, here is the backstory.

Take a look at Listing 1-4. Neither of the two statements terminates in a semicolon. This is perfectly legitimate from a syntactic perspective. As an analogy, consider reading a sentence in plain English. Even if the writer omits the period at the end of a sentence, you can still infer that a sentence ended, because a new paragraph immediately follows.

Listing 1-4. No Semicolons—All Good

```
...
<script>
    console.log("Here is a statement")
    console.log("Here is the last statement")
</script>
...
```

Listing 1-5 is a totally different story. Here we have two statements on the same line. This is not legitimate JavaScript, and problems will occur when you run it. More specifically, you will get a SyntaxError: Unexpected identifier error message in most web browsers. Essentially, it is not clear to the JavaScript runtime where one statement ends and another begins. Back to our analogy: it may well be clear when one paragraph begins and another starts, but the same is not true of a sequence of sentences.

Listing 1-5. Both Statements on the Same Line—NOT Good

```
<script>
    console.log("Here is a statement") console.log("Here is the last statement");
</script>
```

Listing 1-6 shows how you can restore order and overcome the problem in Listing 1-5. As both statements are on the same line, a semicolon makes it clear where one starts and the other ends.

Listing 1-6. Both Statements on the Same Line—All Good

```
<script>
    console.log("Here is a statement"); console.log("Here is the last statement");
</script>
```

As I said, the best way to handle this is to just sidestep it altogether. Use semicolons as a matter of habit and best practice.

It isn't always obvious what a statement or group of statements is supposed to do. With that in mind, it is a good practice to add meaningful comments to your code. JavaScript gives you two ways to do just that: single-line comments and multiline comments. Take a look at Listing 1-7.

Listing 1-7. Using Comments

```
<!DOCTYPE html>
<html>
<head >
    <title>JavaScript Primer</title>
    <script>
      // The lines in this script block execute first
        console.log("I am a statement");
        console.log("I am also a statement");
    </script>
</head>
<body>
<script>
        /*The lines in this script block execute
        after the lines in the script block above*/
    console.log("Here is another statement");
    console.log("Here is the last statement");
</script>
</body>
</html>
```

Listing 1-7 is functionally identical to Listing 1-3, but this version uses comments within each script block. The first uses single-line comments, which are useful for short comments that need not span multiple lines. The second uses the multiline approach. Ideally, you should make sure that your comments say something useful about the purpose and context of your code, something that will help you or others understand why it is there.

Functions

A *function* is a block of JavaScript code that is defined once but may be executed, or invoked, any number of times. Functions are easy to create: just type the keyword `function`, choose a name for your function, and put the function code between a pair of curly braces. See Listing 1-8 for an example of a simple JavaScript function.

Listing 1-8. A Simple Function

```
<!DOCTYPE html>
<html>
<head>
<title>JavaScript Primer</title>
  <script>
    function mySimpleFunction() {
                console.log("Hello");
    }

    mySimpleFunction();
    mySimpleFunction();

  </script>
</head>

<body>

</body>

</html>
```

Here we define a function called mySimpleFunction. We could have named this function mysimplefunction (all lowercase) or even mySIMPLefunCTion (a mixture of upper- and lowercase letters), but best practices dictate that we use an uppercase character at the beginning of each new word (an approach known as camel casing). This makes it much more readable.

With the function now in place, we want to make use of it. Using a function is as simple as typing the function name, followed by parentheses, a process known as *invoking,* or *calling,* the function. Here we invoke mySimpleFunction two times. It isn't a terribly useful function, but it does illustrate the idea that we only need to set up a function once and then reuse it as often as we like. Here is the output:

```
Hello
Hello
```

Parameters and Return Values

Let's look at a function that uses parameters and can return a value. We will name it tripler, because it can triple any number with which it is provided. Our tripler function will define a single parameter, a number, and return a value equal to this number multiplied by three (see Listing 1-9).

Listing 1-9. A Function with Arguments and a Return Value

```
<!DOCTYPE html>
<html>
<head>
  <title>JavaScript Primer</title>
  <script>

    function tripler(numberToTriple) {

        return 3 * numberToTriple;

    }

    console.log(tripler(150));
    console.log(tripler(300));

  </script>
</head>
<body>
</body>
</html>
```

Listing 1-9 shows the `tripler` function in action. First, we define the function. Still keeping things simple, within the function body (the code between the opening and closing curly braces), we immediately return the result of the computed value back to the caller. In this case, there are two callers: one that passes in a value of 150 and another that passes in a value of 300.

The `return` statement is crucial here. It takes care of exiting the function and passing the computed value back to the caller. Equally important is the `numberToTriple` parameter, as it contains the value that we are interested in tripling.

Again, we use the console to show the output. Sure enough, we get the results of calling our function two times, each time with a different argument passed in and a different result returned.

```
450
900
```

■ **Tip**   I just used the term *argument* with regard to the value passed into our function. You may be wondering why I didn't stick with the term *parameter*? Well, I probably could have gotten away with doing that, but in reality, they are subtly different things. Parameters are things defined by functions as variables, while arguments are the values that get passed in to be assigned to these variables.

Types and Variables

Variables are the containers that hold the data with which your application works. Essentially, they are named areas of computer memory in which you can store and retrieve values with which you are working. Listing 1-10 shows you how to declare a variable.

Listing 1-10. Declaring Multiple Variables at Once

```
<!DOCTYPE html>
<html>
<head>
    <title>JavaScript Primer</title>
</head>
<body>
<script>

    var color = "red";
    console.log("The color is " + color);

</script>
</body>
</html>
```

In the preceding listing, we use the var keyword to declare a new variable and then immediately assign it a value of "red". The output below is then, perhaps, unsurprising.

```
The color is red
```

Listing 1-11 provides another example. This time we declare three variables at once and then assign values to each of them afterward.

Listing 1-11. Declaring Multiple Variables at Once

```
<!DOCTYPE html>
<html>
<head>
    <title>JavaScript Primer</title>
</head>
<body>
<script>

    // declare some variables
    var color, size, shape;

    // assign values to them
    color = 'blue';
    size = 'large';
    shape = 'circular';

    console.log("Your widget is the color " + color + " and its size is " + size + ". It is " +
shape + " in shape.");

</script>
</body>
</html>
```

It is common to see multiple variables declared all on the one line, as I have done in Listing 1-11, but you will also see this done with each variable on its own line, as the following code snippet shows:

```
// declare some variables
var color,
    size,
    shape;
```

I prefer the first approach, but this is generally just a matter of taste. Listing 1-11 produces the output following.

```
Your widget is the color blue and its size is large. It is circular in shape.
```

You will notice that each value that we have used so far has been a string value, that is, a series of characters. This is just one of the types that JavaScript supports. Now let's look at the others.

Primitive Types

JavaScript supports a number of primitive types. These types are known as primitive types, as they are the fundamental built-in types that are readily available. Objects, which I discuss in the next section, are generally composed of these primitive types.

Booleans

A *Boolean value* is intended to represent just two possible states: true and false. Here is an example:

```
var isLoggedIn  =  true;
var isMember  =  false;
```

Note that, in both cases, we do not put quotation marks around the values, that is, true and false are not the same as "true" and "false". The latter are string types, not Boolean types.

Interestingly, if you do happen to assign the string "false" to a variable, in Boolean terms, that variable's value will be true. Consider the following examples:

```
isMember  =  "false";
isMember  =  1;
isMember  =  "Hello";
```

Each of these variables has an inherent Boolean value, that is, a quality that leads us to categorize them as *truthy*. That is to say, each of these values represent true. Conversely, each of the following is falsy.

```
isMember  =  "";
isMember  =  0;
isMember  =  -0;
```

Strings

A *string* stores a series of characters, such as "Hello JavaScript." You have two choices when creating strings: you can use single quotation marks or double quotation marks. Both of the variables below are string types.

```
var firstName = "Jane";    // enclosed by double quotation marks
var lastName  = 'Doe';     // enclosed by single quotation marks
```

It doesn't really matter which variation you use, but consistency is good practice. One nice thing about this flexibility is that you can use one within the other. That is, you can use single quotation marks within a string created using double quotation marks, as I do in the following example:

```
// a single quotation mark inside a double quoted string
var opinion = "It's alright";
```

This works both ways, as the following example demonstrates:

```
// double quotation marks inside a single quoted string  var sentence = 'Billy said,
"How are you today?", and smiled.';
```

You can also use the handy backslash to achieve the same thing, regardless of which way you create your strings.

```
// using the backslash to escape single and double quotes
var sentence = "Billy said, \"How are you today?\", and smiled.";
var opinion = 'It\'s alright';
```

In case it is unclear why we have to handle strings in this way, consider the issue with the string following:

```
var bigProblem = "Billy said, "How are you today?", and smiled.";
console.log(bigProblem);
```

This produces the very unpleasant output that follows. As far as JavaScript is concerned, you declared a variable containing the string "Billy said," and then proceeded to type invalid JavaScript code!

```
Uncaught SyntaxError: Unexpected identifier
```

What you should not do is to use single and double quotation marks interchangeably, as I do in the following example:

```
// This is a bad idea!
var badIdea = "This will not end well';
```

Here, I start the string with double quotation marks and end it with single quotation marks—a very bad idea indeed, because this will cause a syntax error.

Numbers

The *number type* is used to represent numbers in JavaScript, both integers and floating-point numbers. JavaScript will look at the value and treat it accordingly. Listing 1-12 uses a simple script to demonstrate this point.

Listing 1-12. Numbers in JavaScript

```
<!DOCTYPE html>
<html>
<head>
    <title>JavaScript Primer</title> </head>
<body>
<script>

    var val1 = 22;
    var val2 = 23;
    console.log(val1 + val2);

    var val3= 22.5;
    var val4 = 23.5;
    console.log(val3 + val4);

    var val5= 50;
    var val6 = .6;
    console.log(val5 + val6);

    // watch out!
    var val7= 25;
    var val8 = "25";
    console.log(val7 + val8);

</script>
</body>
</html>
```

Looking at the output below, you can see that JavaScript is mostly doing just what you would expect; however, you will see something that may appear unusual on the last line of output.

```
4
46
50.6
2525
```

If you look at Listing 1-12 again, you will see that the variable val8 was actually declared as a string. JavaScript inferred what you intended, and it coerced val7 into type string also. Consequently, you end up with two strings concatenated together (which is how the + operator acts when used on strings). I will talk a little more about JavaScript type conversion shortly.

Undefined and Null

JavaScript has two subtly different types to represent the idea of missing values: undefined and null.

```
var myName;
console.log(myName);
```

Here we have a variable called myName to which we have assigned no value. When we print the value of this variable to the console, we get the following result:

```
undefined
```

JavaScript uses undefined to represent a variable that has been declared but has not yet been assigned a value. This is subtly different from the following situation:

```
var myName = null;
console.log(myName)
```

In this case, I specifically assigned the value of null. Consequently, the output is as follows:

```
null
```

From these examples, it is clear that undefined and null are two distinct types: undefined is a *type* (undefined), while null is an *object*. The concept of null and undefined can be rather tricky in JavaScript, but as a general rule of thumb, you should favor using null whenever you have to declare a variable to which you are not ready to assign a value.

JavaScript Operators

JavaScript supports all of the standard operators that you would expect to find in a programming language. Table 1-1 lists some of the more commonly used operators.

Table 1-1. *Commonly Used JavaScript Operators*

Operator	Description
++, --	Pre- or post-increment and decrement
+, -, *, /, %	Addition, subtraction, multiplication, division, remainder
<, <=, >, >=	Less than, less than or equal to, more than, more than or equal to
==, !=	Equality and inequality tests
===, !==	Identity and nonidentity tests
&&, ||	Logical AND and OR (|| is used to coalesce null values)
=	Assignment
+	String concatenation

Some of these operators may make intuitive sense, others perhaps not. Let's write a simple program to look at how they behave. There are a couple of cases in which we will look a bit closer at some of these operators, so I will omit them in Listing 1-13 and deal with them shortly afterward.

Listing 1-13. Common Operators in Action

```
<!DOCTYPE html>
<html>
<head>
    <title>JavaScript Primer</title>
</head>
<body>
<script>

    console.log("Doing assignment");
    var myName = "Catie";
    console.log(myName);

    console.log("Doing arithmetic");
    console.log(5 + 5);    // 10
    console.log(5 - 5);    // 0
    console.log(5 * 5);    // 25
    console.log(5 / 5);    // 1
    console.log(5 % 5);    // 0
    console.log(11 % 10); // 1

    console.log("Doing comparisons");
    console.log(11 > 10);   // true
    console.log(11 < 10);   // false
    console.log(10 >= 10); // true
    console.log(11 <= 10); // false

    console.log("Doing string concatenation");
    console.log(myName + " Grant"); // "Catie Grant"

    console.log("Doing boolean logic");
    console.log(true && true);  // true
    console.log(true && false); // false
    console.log(true || true);  // true
    console.log(true || false); // true

</script>
</body>
</html>
```

Listing 1-13 shows the output of some basic operations. I've put the output in comments next to each line of code, to make it easier to reconcile. You can use Table 1-1 to clarify your understanding of how each produces its respective output.

Equality vs. Identity

I mentioned previously that I'd like to cover some of these operators as special cases. The identity (===) and equality (==) operators are one such special case. These operators look similar, and they can even appear to behave similarly, but, in fact, they are significantly different.

When performing comparisons, the equality operator (==) will attempt to make the data types the same before proceeding. On the other hand, the identity operator (===) requires both data types to be the same, as a prerequisite. This is one of those concepts best conveyed through code, as shown in Listing 1-14.

Listing 1-14. Converting Types and Then Comparing

```
<!DOCTYPE html>
<html>
<head>
    <title>JavaScript Primer</title>
</head>
<body>
<script>

    var valueOne = 3;
    var valueTwo = "3";
    if (valueOne == valueTwo) {
        console.log("ValueOne and ValueTwo are the same");
    } else {
        console.log("ValueOne and ValueTwo are NOT the same");
    }

</script>
</body>
</html>
```

I'm not sure what you expect to see in the output that follows, given that we are comparing the number 3 to the string value "3". You may or may not be surprised, but these values are considered to be the same.

```
ValueOne and ValueTwo are the same
```

The reason why the == operator reasons that "3" and 3 are the same is because it actually coverts the operands (the values either side of the == operator) to the same type *before* it does the comparison. However, if we change the operator to an identity operator, as shown here, we see quite different output:

```
if (valueOne === valueTwo)
```

```
ValueOne and ValueTwo are NOT the same
```

Since we used the === operator on this occasion, and because this operator does not do any type conversion, we see that the string value "3" and the number 3 are not the same after all.

When in doubt, a relatively safe choice is simply to use the identity operator (===) as a matter of habit. Of course, the safest choice is to familiarize yourself with the differences, so that you know what is actually happening under the hood.

JavaScript is very flexible with types, and it allows you significant freedoms, but the tradeoff is that what is going on behind the scenes is not always obvious. For example, you have already seen that the + operator performs double duty: it can do addition and it can also do string concatenation. With that in mind, examine the following code snippet. Can you predict its output?

```
// Will this produce the number 2 or the string "11"?
console.log("1" + 1);
```

The output is:

11

From this, we can deduce that JavaScript must have converted the number value to a string value and performed a concatenation operation, as opposed to an addition operation.

At times, as you might imagine, we want some control over types. Fortunately, JavaScript comes with the right tools. Table 1-2 shows just a few of the tools you have at your disposal.

Table 1-2. *A Few Built-in Type-Related Utilities*

Function / Operator	Description
typeof	Allows you to ask the data type of its operand. It can provide the following values:
	"number"
	"string"
	"boolean"
	"object"
	"undefined"
	null
parseInt	The parseInt() function parses a string and returns a number. If it cannot return a number, it will return NaN (Not a Number).
toString	Converts a value, such as a number, to a string
isNaN	The isNaN function can tell you if a given value is *not* a number. For example, isNaN('three') will return true; isNaN(3) will return false.

Listing 1-15 shows each of these in action.

Listing 1-15. Type Conversion Examples

```
<!DOCTYPE html>
<html>
<head>
   <title>JavaScript Primer</title>
</head>
<body>
```

```
<script>

        // create a string variable
        var myStringType = "22";
        // use the handy typeof operator to
        // confirm the type is indeed string
        console.log(typeof myStringType );

        // create a number variable
        var myNumberType = 45;
        // use the handy typeof operator to
        // confirm the type is indeed number
        console.log(typeof myNumberType );

        // Now let's convert myStringType to
        // a number type using the parseInt()
        // method
        var myStringType = parseInt(myStringType);
        // confirm the type is indeed number
        console.log(typeof myStringType );

        // finally, let's convert the myNumberType
        // to a string
        var myNumberType = myNumberType.toString();
        // confirm the type is indeed string
        console.log(typeof myNumberType );

</script>
</body>
</html>
```

It's well worth exploring these built-in functions and others like them. JavaScript's dynamic type system is often a good thing, but it does mean that any serious JavaScript programmer has to become accustomed to how types are being managed behind the scenes.

Pre- vs. Post-Increment

I will finish this section by looking at the last of the special cases: the pre- and post-increment operators (++) and their decrement (--) counterparts.

These operators are relatively easy to understand on the surface. Essentially, they are a more compact way of performing operations, such as the following:

```
myNumber = myNumber + 1;
myNumber += myNumber;
```

Another way that you can achieve the same result as the preceding two techniques is as follows:

```
myNumber = ++myNumber;
```

In all cases, the value of myNumber increments by 1. Take special note here that the preceding increment operator appears *before* the variable myNumber. In this case, we refer to it as a *pre*-increment. A *post*-increment, as you might expect, would look like this:

```
myNumber = myNumber++;
```

This seems straightforward enough, so why am I treating these operators as a special case? Because, potentially, there is a serious mistake that can be made when using them. This is demonstrated in Listing 1-16.

Listing 1-16. Pre- vs. Post-Increment Behavior

```
<!DOCTYPE html>
<html>
<head >
    <title>JavaScript Primer</title>
</head>
<body>
<script>

    // Pre-increment
    var myNumber = 1;
    myNumber = myNumber + 1;
    myNumber = ++myNumber;
    console.log("Pre-increment result is " + myNumber);

    // Post-increment
    var myOtherNumber = 1;
    myOtherNumber = myOtherNumber + 1;
    myOtherNumber = myOtherNumber++;
    console.log("Post increment result is " + myOtherNumber);

</script>
</body>
</html>
```

Read through Listing 1-15, and see if you can figure out why the output is as shown following. The answer lies in the nature of how or, rather, when these operators perform their work.

```
Pre-increment result is  3
Post-increment result is 2
```

If you found it odd that the post-increment result was 2 instead of 3, here's why: the post increment operation happens *after* the assignment operation. Let me clarify this by breaking it down a bit.

```
myNumber = ++myNumber;
```

Reading the preceding code snippet in plain English, you might say this: "Increment the current value of myNumber, and then store it into the variable myNumber." However, if you look at the post-increment variation of this:

```
myNumber = myNumber++;
```

you now have to interpret this as *"Store the current value of* myNumber *into* myNumber, *and then increment the value."* In this case, the net result is that the increment happens after the assignment operation, so the myNumber variable never actually receives the updated (incremented) value. The same principle applies to the pre- and post-decrement (--) operators.

Working with Objects

Objects are often used as containers for data, but they can be home to functions too. They are a particularly versatile aspect of the JavaScript language, and it is very important to get a decent handle on this concept.

Creating Objects

Let's start our brief look at objects by seeing how they are created. Listing 1-17 demonstrates the usual way to create an object.

Listing 1-17. Creating Objects

```
<!DOCTYPE html>
<html>
<head>
    <title>JavaScript Primer</title>
</head>
<body>
<script>

    // Example 1
    var myFirstObject = {};
    myFirstObject.firstName = "Andrew";
    myFirstObject.lastName = "Grant";
    console.log(myFirstObject.firstName);

    // Example 2
    var mySecondObject = {
        firstName: "Andrew",
        lastName: "Grant"
    };
    console.log(mySecondObject.firstName);

    // Example 3
    var myThirdObject = new Object();
    myThirdObject.firstName = "Andrew";
    myThirdObject.lastName = "Grant";
    console.log(myThirdObject.firstName);

</script>
</body>
</html>
```

Listing 1-17 shows a few different ways of creating objects. I tend not to use or come across the new Object() technique very much (commented with Example 3 in the listing), and I think you will see the other two approaches used a lot more. Examples 1, 2, and 3 all do the same thing: they create an object, add a couple of properties to it, and assign some values to those properties. Each example logs to the console to produce the following output:

```
Andrew
Andrew
Andrew
```

■ **Note**   You can think of properties as variables defined on objects. However, in the world of object-oriented programming, which I don't cover in this book, there are far better definitions.

Reading and Modifying an Object's Properties

Changing the values of properties can be done in a couple of ways. Listing 1-18 demonstrates accessing and changing object values.

Listing 1-18. Accessing and Changing Object Values

```html
<!DOCTYPE html>
<html>
<head>
    <title>JavaScript Primer</title>
</head>
<body>
<script>

    var myFirstObject = {};
    myFirstObject.firstName = "Andrew";
    console.log(myFirstObject.firstName);

    myFirstObject.firstName = "Monica";
    console.log(myFirstObject.firstName);

    myFirstObject["firstName"] = "Catie";
    console.log(myFirstObject["firstName"]);

</script>
</body>
</html>
```

As the following output demonstrates, we start off by setting a value of Andrew on the firstName property; shortly thereafter, we change that value to Monica. On both occasions, we use dot syntax, that is, the object name, followed by a dot and then the property name. Shortly afterward, we change it yet again, but this time, we use associative array syntax. This syntax requires us to use the object name and then to specify the property name within brackets.

```
Andrew
Monica
Catie
```

Which approach you use can often be a matter of preference, but associative array syntax has some nifty benefits. For example, you can use a variable name inside the brackets, which makes for some very handy dynamic behavior. Listing 1-19 provides a quick example of this.

Listing 1-19. Associative Array

```
<!DOCTYPE html>
<html>
<head>
    <title>JavaScript Primer</title>
</head>
<body>
<script>

    var myFirstObject = {};
    myFirstObject["firstName"] = "Catie";

    console.log(myFirstObject["firstName"]);

    // Here we use a variable to determine which
    // property we are accessing
    var propertyName = "firstName";
    myFirstObject[propertyName] = "Christopher";
    console.log(myFirstObject["firstName"]);

</script>
</body>
</html>
```

The important part of Listing 1-18 is where we update the firstName property using the previously declared propertyName variable. Using dot syntax, you cannot do this. The output is as follows:

```
Catie
Christopher
```

▪ **Note** Be careful when using associative array syntax. If you make a typo and write, say, ["firstNme"] instead of ["firstName"], you will actually create on the object a new property called firstNme.

Adding Methods to Objects

We looked at functions earlier, and now we are going to look at methods. Here's the good news: methods and functions are so similar, you are already most of the way there. Let's look at the example shown in Listing 1-20.

Listing 1-20. An Object with a Method

```
<!DOCTYPE html>
<html>
<head>
    <title>JavaScript Primer</title>
</head>
<body>
<script>

    var myCleverObject = {
        firstName: "Andrew",
        age: 21,
        myInfo: function () {
            console.log("My name is " + this.firstName + ". ");
            console.log("My age is " + this.age + ".");
        }
    };

    myCleverObject.myInfo();

</script>
</body>
</html>
```

If you look through Listing 1-20, you will see that it isn't really anything special, until you get to the myInfo property. This property has a value just like any other property, but it just so happens to be a function. The last line shows it being called through the object reference.

A function attached to an object in this manner is known as a *method*. Why is that? The short and simple answer is that, in reality, they are subtly different things, both in how JavaScript treats them and how you, as a developer, are supposed to use them.

Did you notice that inside the myInfo method we refer to name as this.name? Using the special this keyword, you get access to other properties of the same object. Essentially, this is a reference to the current object. (Some of you may be familiar with other languages in which something like this exists under the guise of Me or self.) Here is the output:

```
My name is Andrew.
My age is 21.
```

I want to make a minor change to the preceding listing. Here is a snippet of the affected area, the myInfo method:

```
myInfo: function () {
    console.log("My name is " + firstName + ". ");
    console.log("My age is " + age + ".");
}
```

Everything is identical, except for the fact that I removed the this keyword from firstName and age. This is an example of *what not to do*. As the following output shows, my browser didn't like it one bit.

```
Uncaught ReferenceError: firstName is not defined
```

The moral of the story is this (no pun intended): make sure that you access the current object's properties via the this keyword, if you want to avoid unpredictable results.

I cannot delve much into object-oriented programming techniques here, as this is a huge topic that would fill many books in its own right. However, although I didn't touch upon it much here, it is worth knowing that JavaScript does support this paradigm quite well, should you wish to explore it further.

Enumerating Properties

You can use a for in loop to enumerate an object's properties. This is an easy way to interrogate any object, and it has many other uses as well. Listing 1-21 provides an example of a for in loop.

Listing 1-21. The for in Loop

```
<!DOCTYPE html>
<html>
<head>
    <title>JavaScript Primer</title>
</head>
<body>
<script>


    var myObject = {
        firstname: "Andrew",
        surname:"Grant",
        age: 21
    };


    for (var prop in myObject) {
        console.log(myObject[prop]);
    }

</script>
</body>
</html>
```

Listing 1-21 uses a for in loop to print each property of myObject to the console. It can be extremely handy at times, though this example isn't exactly awe-inspiring. All we do here is use the variable prop, which changes with each pass through the loop, to print the property's value to the console.

```
Andrew
Grant
21
```

Remember the use of the associative array syntax that we discussed earlier? myObject[prop] is a good example of where this technique is needed.

Control Flow

Generally speaking, JavaScript is read by the browser line by line, unless you tell it otherwise, using, for example, a loop or branch statement. *Looping* is the ability to repeat the execution of a block of code a number of times; whereas *branching* is the ability to jump to one block of code or potentially some other block of code.

Loops

Let's start off with loops. Arguably the most common loop structure in JavaScript is the for loop. The for loop can seem complicated at first, but it's not difficult to use, once you understand what it is composed of.

There are four key parts to a for loop:

1. *Counter variable*. This is something that is created and usually used only in the for loop. Its main task is to keep count of how many times the loop has been entered.

2. *Conditional logic*. This is where the decision is made on whether or not the for loop should continue.

3. *Counter variable*. This is usually incremented, or otherwise altered, after every loop.

4. *Code block*. This is the actual block of code that is executed at each pass through the loop.

With these explanations in mind, let's examine Listing 1-22, which shows the for loop in action. I hope you will be able to read through this and relate each part back to the preceding points.

Listing 1-22. The for Loop in Action

```
<!DOCTYPE html>
<html>
<head>
    <title>JavaScript Primer</title>
</head>
<body>
<script>

    console.log("Looping started");
    // set up the for loop here
    for (i = 0; i < 5; i++) {
        console.log("The current value of i is " + i + ". We will loop again because " + i + "
is less than 5");
    }
```

```
        console.log("Looping finished");

</script>
</body>
</html>
```

The first thing we do is to print Looping started to the console. Then we enter the for loop. We enter the for loop because of the conditional check, the bit that reads i < 5. Well, i (which is the counter) starts off at 0, so i < 5 evaluates to true. Only when i < 5 evaluates to false will the loop end and continue on to the next line of code, in this case, the code that prints Looping finished to the console.

So, why would the variable i ever change its original value of 0? This is because each time the loop executes, it also carries out the i++ logic. So, the counter goes up at each pass and eventually the loop ends.

The results follow. We will see the for loop in action again when I cover JavaScript arrays shortly.

```
Looping started
The current value of i is 0. We will loop again because 0 is less than 5
The current value of i is 1. We will loop again because 1 is less than 5
The current value of i is 2. We will loop again because 2 is less than 5
The current value of i is 3. We will loop again because 3 is less than 5
The current value of i is 4. We will loop again because 4 is less than 5
Looping finished
```

The while loop is a somewhat simpler version of the for loop. It doesn't require as much setup, but it isn't quite as powerful (at least not without extra work). The basic structure of a while loop looks like this:

```
while( some value is true){
        execture this block of code
    }
```

The preceding isn't real code, of course, but Listing 1-23 provides a basic demo of the while loop.

Listing 1-23. The while Loop in Action

```
<!DOCTYPE html>
<html>
<head>
    <title>JavaScript Primer</title>
</head>
<body>
<script>

    var i = 0;
    while (i < 10) {
        console.log("The value of i is " + i);
        i++;
    }

</script>
</body>
</html>
```

You might consider the while loop to be a less structured version of the for loop. Indeed, you can happily program in JavaScript, forever ignoring the while loop by exclusively using the for loop. However, you will come across many situations in which using a while loop can be very convenient and much more concise.

Conditional Statements

Conditional statements allow you to implement "fork in the road" logic. That is, JavaScript can execute a statement, or statements, if a specified condition is true. You can also execute a statement, or statements, if this condition is false.

Is this user logged in? Yes? Let him/her see this data. No? Then send him/her to the login page. Listing 1-24 demonstrates how to write this kind of logic in JavaScript.

Listing 1-24. JavaScripts if/else in Action

```
<!DOCTYPE html>
<html>
<head>
    <title>JavaScript Primer</title>
</head>
<body>
<script>

    var userIsLoggedIn = false;

    if(userIsLoggedIn){
        console.log("Welcome back - sending you to some very private data");
    }else{
        console.log("Sorry - access denied");
    }

</script>
</body>
</html>
```

By assigning false to the userIsLoggedIn variable, we are setting up a pretend user that we can consider to be not logged in, just so we have something with which to work. Next is the if(userIsLoggedIn) portion of the code. The if statement expects whatever expression or variable is placed between these parentheses to evaluate to either true or false. It will only execute the code in the associated code block if it finds a value of true. Should it find a value of false, it will execute the block of code within the else statement.

I hope the following results will make perfect sense.

```
Sorry - access denied
```

You do not have to provide an else statement if your program doesn't require it. Also, you can nest if and if/else statements inside of each other. Listing 1-25 demonstrates both of these ideas.

Listing 1-25. Nested Conditional Logic

```
<!DOCTYPE html>
<html>
<head>
    <title>JavaScript Primer</title>
</head>
<body>
<script>

    var userIsLoggedIn = false;
    var userIsVIP = true;

    if(userIsLoggedIn){

        console.log("Welcome back - showing you some very private data");

        if(userIsVIP){
            console.log("You are entitled to a 25% discount!");
        }else{
            console.log("You are entitled to a 10% discount!");
        }

    }

</script>
</body>
</html>
```

This listing is similar to Listing 1-23, the difference being that there is no else counterpart to the if statement. In these cases, when the condition evaluates to false, no action is taken at all. Also, we use a nested if/else statement. So, if the user is logged in, we ask yet another question: is this user a VIP member? As userIsVIP evaluates to true, we give this member a much higher discount.

```
Welcome back - showing you to some very private data
You are entitled to a 25% discount!
```

Working with Arrays

JavaScript arrays are used to store multiple values in a single variable. JavaScript arrays are quite flexible in that you can store variables of different types within them. (Some languages do not allow for this.) Arrays allow you to work, based on the position of contained items, by using a numeric index. Listing 1-26 is a basic example of creating an array and adding values to it.

Listing 1-26. Working with Arrays

```
<!DOCTYPE html>
<html>
<head>
    <title>JavaScript Primer</title>
</head>
<body>
<script>

    var myArray = [];
    myArray[0] = "Andrew";
    myArray[1] = "Monica";
    myArray[2] = "Catie";
    myArray[3] = "Jenna";
    myArray[4] = "Christopher";

    console.log("Item at index 0: " + myArray[0]);
    console.log("Item at index 1: " + myArray[1]);
    console.log("Item at index 2: " + myArray[2]);
    console.log("Item at index 3: " + myArray[3]);
    console.log("Item at index 4: " + myArray[4]);

</script>
</body>
</html>
```

Here, we create an array called myArray and populate it with five string values. As arrays in JavaScript are zero-based, we start off at zero and finish up at four, for a total of five items. The results follow:

```
Item at index 0: Andrew
Item at index 1: Monica
Item at index 2: Catie
Item at index 3: Jenna
Item at index 4: Christopher
```

It can be somewhat tricky trying to keep the index straight, that is, keeping track of which item is at which position. JavaScript provides the Array.length property, so that you have something with which to work. Listing 1-27 provides an example using the length property.

Listing 1-27. Using the Length Property

```
...

var myArray = [];
myArray[myArray.length] = "Andrew";
myArray[myArray.length] = "Monica";
myArray[myArray.length] = "Catie";
myArray[myArray.length] = "Jenna";
myArray[myArray.length] = "Christopher";
```

```
// Display the first item
console.log("The first item is: " + myArray[0]);
// Dislay the last item
console.log("The last item is: " + myArray[myArray.length - 1]);
```

...

Listing 1-27 is similar to Listing 1-26, but instead of hard-coding the index values, we use the length property to calculate the current position. Note the need to cater to the zero-based nature of arrays. Accessing the last item in the array requires us to subtract 1 from the length property.

```
The first item is: Andrew
The last item is: Christopher
```

Array Literals

The manner in which we have gone about creating arrays so far might be considered the long way. I will show you an alternative way, which is more concise and, arguably, more readable when you are creating an array and populating it with values all in one go round. Instead of doing this:

```
var myArray = [];
    myArray[0] = "Andrew";
    myArray[1] = "Monica";
    myArray[2] = "Catie";
    myArray[3] = "Jenna";
    myArray[4] = "Christopher";
```

you can achieve the same result doing this:

```
var myArray = ["Andrew","Monica","Catie","Jenna","Christopher"];
```

This is certainly the style I prefer in most cases. I chose the first approach mainly because it was more demonstrative of the index-based nature of arrays.

Enumerating and Modifying Array Values

The usual way of enumerating an array is to use a for loop, which I covered in the "Control Flow" section earlier in this chapter. Listing 1-28 shows this approach in action.

Listing 1-28. Enumerating an Array

```
var myArray = ["Andrew","Monica","Catie","Jenna","Christopher"];

for(var i = 0; i < myArray.length; i++) {
    console.log(myArray[i]);
}
```

The output of Listing 1-28 follows:

```
Andrew
Monica
Catie
Jenna
Christopher
```

As you can see, this approach hinges on the use of the Array.length property, looping through from 0 to the very last index in the array.

Modifying array values is the same as modifying the values of any other variable, with the exception that you need to know its location within the array. Listing 1-29 shows how we can update the entire array by adding the family surname to each item.

Listing 1-29. Modifying Array Values

```
<!DOCTYPE html>
<html>
<head>
    <title>JavaScript Primer</title>
</head>
<body>
<script>

    var myArray = ["Andrew","Monica","Catie","Jenna","Christopher"];

    console.log("Before: ", myArray);

    for(var i = 0; i < myArray.length; i++) {
        myArray[i] = myArray[i] + " Grant";
    }

    console.log("After: ", myArray);

</script>
</body>
</html>
```

The most important part of this listing is myArray[i] = myArray[i] + " Grant";. All we do here is append the family surname to the existing value at position i at each pass through the loop. Notice that I also log the entire array to the console both before and after I modify the array's contents. Passing the array to console.log() is a handy way to dump the contents of the entire array for inspection. The output is as follows:

```
Before: ["Andrew", "Monica", "Catie", "Jenna", "Christopher"]
After: ["Andrew Grant", "Monica Grant", "Catie Grant", "Jenna Grant", "Christopher Grant"]
```

Callbacks

Callbacks can be a bit confusing, both for new programmers and for seasoned professionals alike (at least for those new to the functional programming style upon which callbacks are based). The key to enlightenment, I think, is first to understand that functions are objects that can be passed around just like any other value in JavaScript.

Let's step through this slowly. Listing 1-30 provides an example that shows how you can create a variable and then store a function in that variable.

Listing 1-30. Storing a Function Reference in a Variable: Part 1

```
<!DOCTYPE html>
<html>
<head>
    <title>JavaScript Primer</title>
</head>
<body>
<script>

    var myFunctionReference = function () {
        console.log('callbacks part 1')
    }

    myFunctionReference();
    myFunctionReference;
    myFunctionReference();

</script>

</body>
</html>
```

Listing 1-30 is quite short, but a particularly important concept is illustrated within it. We start off by declaring a variable called myFunctionReference, in which we store a function or, rather, a reference to a function.

You might think that the function looks a little odd; it has no name. That's OK because it is stored in the variable myFunctionReference, so when we want to use this function, we can use the parentheses to call it.

Look closely at the last three lines. In two cases, I use the parentheses, but in one case, I do not. In the case in which I do not, the function reference is not called (or invoked). It is the parentheses, also known as the *call operator*, that cause the function to run. Here are the results:

```
callbacks part 1
callbacks part 1
```

This idea that functions are themselves values that can be assigned to variables is important. Listing 1-31 is done in a way that may (or may not) seem more intuitive, if you have not used anonymous functions (functions without a name) before.

Listing 1-31. Storing a Function Reference in a Variable: Part 2

```
<!DOCTYPE html>
<html>
<head>
    <title>JavaScript Primer</title>
</head>
<body>
<script>

    function anotherFunctionReference() {
        console.log('callbacks part 2');
    }

    var x = anotherFunctionReference;
    x();
    anotherFunctionReference();
    x();
    anotherFunctionReference();
    x();

</script>

</body>
</html>
```

Listing 1-31 defines a function and stores a reference to that function in two separate steps. This time around, the function has a name. We can use both its name and the reference to call it. The following output confirms this.

```
callbacks part 2
callbacks part 2
callbacks part 2
callbacks part 2
callbacks part 2
```

Keeping in mind the idea of functions as values that can be assigned to variables, we now look at callbacks. *Callbacks* are just functions that you pass to some other function, so that they can be called at some later point. The reasons you might want to do this may vary, but it is generally due to some circumstance for which you must wait some time before your function has enough context to execute meaningfully, such as with Ajax calls to a web server.

▨ **Note**   Ajax allows web pages to be updated asynchronously by exchanging small amounts of data with the server behind the scenes. This makes it possible to update parts of a web page without reloading the whole page. One of the ways AngularJS supports this is through its $http service, which we will see more of in Chapter 7.

Listing 1-32 is a little contrived, but it shows the general idea of how callbacks work.

Listing 1-32. A Simple Callback in Action

```
<!DOCTYPE html>
<html>
<head>
    <title>JavaScript Primer</title>
</head>
<body>
<script>

    var actionsToTakeWhenServerHasResponded = function () {
        console.log('The server just responded!')
    }

    function communicateWithServer(callback) {

        callback();
    }

    communicateWithServer(actionsToTakeWhenServerHasResponded);


</script>

</body>
</html>
```

Here we have a variable called actionsToTakeWhenServerHasResponded. This variable is a function reference. On the next line down, we have a function called communicateWithServer. The thing to take note of here is that this function takes an argument, which we have named callback, which it expects to be a function reference.

Finally, on the last line, we call the communicateWithServer function and pass it the actionsToTakeWhenServerHasResponded variable. I hope that you can see that inside our communicateWithServer function, our actionsToTakeWhenServerHasResponded function is executed through the callback reference. See the following results:

```
The server just responded!
```

For the most part, this example represents the nature of callbacks. One thing it doesn't do very well is demonstrate time passing as the communicateWithServer does some presumably lengthy task. This is really the point of callbacks—your program can continue to execute as opposed to sitting idle waiting for some lengthy process to finish. Here is a code snippet that shows how this might look in action:

```
console.log('1')

$http.post('/ http://someurl.com/someService ', data).success(function () {
    console.log('2')
});

console.log('3')
```

The interesting part of this example is the success method. It takes a function as an argument. We didn't bother to store the function in a variable this time. It is created right there in the method call (a very common technique). The $http.post() method has to call a server and wait for a response. At some later point, with all going well, the success method will execute the callback function that we passed to it. This process takes, typically, at least a couple of seconds or so. Have a look at how the output for such a scenario would look.

```
1
3
2
```

The key thing to observe here is that 3 comes before 2 in the output. This is because the callback function, which contains the console.log('2') statement, takes place at some point in the future. Thanks to the power of callbacks, your program doesn't have to wait around; it continues executing as normal, happy in the knowledge that there will be a "call back" later.

JSON

JavaScript Object Notation, or *JSON*, is a lightweight data-interchange format. Essentially, it is way of representing data in a way that is much more compact than XML yet still relatively human and totally machine-readable. If you need to send data from place to place, or even store it somewhere, JSON is often a good choice.

Because JSON is JavaScript (well, a subset of JavaScript, to be precise), it is easy to work with. Unlike XML, it is considerably faster over the wire. I won't labor too much on JSON, but I will show you what it looks like. Listing 1-33 shows a sample of JSON data.

Listing 1-33. Sample JSON Data

```
{
    "firstName": "John",
    "lastName": "Smith",
    "address": {
        "streetAddress": "21 2nd Street",
        "city": "New York",
        "state": "NY",
        "postalCode": 10021
    },
    "phoneNumbers": [
        "212 555-1234",
        "646 555-4567"
    ]
}
```

I covered JavaScript objects earlier, so I hope this will look familiar. This is essentially a JavaScript object with a bunch of properties representing contact data for a John Smith. firstName and lastName have simple string values. The address property is itself represented as an object, and the phoneNumbers property is an array.

The same thing in XML is considerably more verbose, relatively difficult to manipulate in JavaScript, and more memory- and storage-intensive. Listing 1-34 shows the JSON from Listing 1-33 represented as XML.

Listing 1-34. The JSON from Listing 1-32 Represented as XML

```
<?xml version="1.0" encoding="UTF-8" ?>
<contact>
    <firstName>John</firstName>
    <lastName>Smith</lastName>
    <address>
        <streetAddress>21 2nd Street</streetAddress>
        <city>New York</city>
        <state>NY</state>
        <postalCode>10021</postalCode>
    </address>
    <phoneNumbers>
        <phoneNumber>212 555-1234</phoneNumber>
        <phoneNumber>646 555-4567</phoneNumber>
    </phoneNumbers>
</contact>
```

It's important to keep in mind that JSON is an alternative to XML, not a replacement. XML has its advantages too: it is more self-descriptive and arguably more human-readable than JSON. That being said, when wearing your JavaScript hat, you will very likely come across JSON much more often, as it is heavily used in many common scenarios, such as communicating with back-end servers.

Summary

This whirlwind tour of JavaScript won't make you an expert, but I hope it has been a useful refresher or a quick introduction. We looked at core language features, such as statements, functions, arrays, and objects. We will be using these features throughout the rest of the book. Where it is helpful to do so, I will include some handy tips and notes that elaborate on these topics and others. This should prove particularly useful for readers who are tackling the JavaScript learning curve somewhat parallel to AngularJS.

CHAPTER 2

The Basics of AngularJS

JavaScript is an important language for web developers—one that is nearly impossible to ignore. It's a language that was created for the relatively simple purpose of adding basic interactivity to web pages. However, it has risen to mainstream importance, and it is used today to build large and sophisticated web applications.

Why We Need Frameworks

You may develop some appreciation of why frameworks such as AngularJS exist, by considering that JavaScript was not originally created with today's much more complex requirements in mind. In fact, in many respects, JavaScript was adapted to this purpose because it was there. It was already widely supported in web browsers, and many developers knew how to use it.

JavaScript sometimes gets a bad rap; it isn't everyone's favorite language. I personally enjoy using it and find that I can work around the things that I perceive as shortcomings; nevertheless, I totally understand why some developers don't feel the same way as I do, particularly those who have not had the chance to warm up to its strengths. I think it is fair to say that JavaScript has many great features, but it is equally fair to say that it is missing a few features—ones that developers feel are vital.

Given its humble beginnings and perceived shortcomings, is JavaScript really ideal for developing modern web applications? It certainly is. As a relatively easy-to-learn language with almost ubiquitous support, it is extremely well suited to the task.

Here's a better question: Is JavaScript ideal for developing applications that require modularity, testability, and developer productivity? The short and simple answer to a question such as this is no, not really. At least not "out of the box." The makers of JavaScript simply didn't have these requirements in mind when it was conceived. However, today we have a proliferation of frameworks and libraries designed to help us with such things. The general idea is that we want to be more productive and that we want to write code, often in response to unreasonably tight deadlines, that we can easily maintain and reuse. This is why we need frameworks.

Each framework achieves its (sometimes significantly different) objectives in a variety of ways and to varying degrees. For example, the popular jQuery framework addresses direct Document Object Model (DOM) manipulation extremely well, but it doesn't really help out much when it comes to keeping your code structured and organized. To be fair, jQuery is more of a library than a full-fledged framework, so this really relates more to my point about varying objectives and degrees.

With regard to front-end web development, AngularJS addresses many, if not all, of the issues developers face when using JavaScript on its own, and it does so in a very elegant and comprehensive way.

There often isn't a right or wrong framework, by the way, because much of what constitutes right may depend on the kind of project on which you are working, your current skills and experience, and your personal preferences. That being said, I personally believe that AngularJS is a great all-around framework, which is definitely among the best available.

■ **Note**   AngularJS comes bundled with a trimmed-down version of jQuery called jqLite. Generally speaking, however, it is better to do things the "Angular Way." You will learn a lot more about what that means as the book progresses.

What Is a Framework?

Before exploring AngularJS in depth, let us consider exactly what AngularJS is. What do we mean by a "framework," and why would we want to use one? Might it be a good idea not to use one? Might it even be a good idea to develop our own instead?

The dictionary definition tells us that a framework is "an essential supporting structure." That sums up AngularJS very nicely, although AngularJS is much more than that. AngularJS is a large and helpful community, an ecosystem in which you can find new tools and utilities, an ingenious way of solving common problems, and, for many, a new and refreshing way of thinking about application structure and design.

We could, if we wanted to make life harder for ourselves, write our own framework. Realistically, however, for most of us, this just isn't viable. It almost goes without saying that you need the support of some kind of framework, and that this framework almost certainly should be something other than your own undocumented (or less than well understood) ideas and thoughts on how things should be done. A good framework, such as AngularJS, is already well tested and well understood by others. Keep in mind that one day others may inherit your code, be on your team, or otherwise need to benefit from the structure and support a framework provides.

The use of frameworks isn't uncommon; many programmers from all walks of life rely on them. Business application developers use frameworks, such as the Microsoft Entity Framework, to ease their pain and speed up development when building database-related applications. For example, Java programmers use the LibGDX framework to help them create games. (We all need a little help.)

I hope I have sold you on the need for a framework and, more specifically, the fact that AngularJS is a great choice. Now, I will spend the rest of this book getting you up to speed as quickly as possible, while putting you on a solid footing to go further than I can take you within its pages. AngularJS is not difficult to learn, and, if you are like me, you will enjoy its unique approach and its knack for making the complex seem considerably less so.

Downloading and Installing AngularJS

Downloading and installing AngularJS is easy, takes very little time, and doesn't require your credit card. It is completely free of charge (under the MIT license).

To download AngularJS, head on over to `http://angularjs.org` and follow these steps:

1.   Create a folder on your computer called BeginningAngularJS. Inside this folder, create a subfolder called js to contain your JavaScript files.

2.   On the AngularJS home page, click the Download button. You will see a dialog box like the one shown in Figure 2-1.

Figure 2-1. *The AngularJS download options dialog*

3. You want the 1.2.x-minified version, so make sure that you choose *1.2.x (legacy)* for the branch option and *Minified* for the build option.

4. Click the Download button to start the download process.

5. Once the download has completed, move the downloaded file, `angular.min.js`, into the js folder that you created earlier (assuming you did not save it there directly).

6. That's it! You just downloaded and installed AngularJS.

Throughout this book, I will assume that you have followed the preceding steps when I refer to file system locations and folder names. If you are comfortable with the Content Delivery Network (CDN), and prefer to use it, feel free to do so. Likewise, if your preference is to use the non-minified version of the AngularJS library, go right ahead. This won't affect the output of any of the code listings (assuming that you have things set up correctly otherwise).

■ **Note** Content Delivery Networks are a great place to host JavaScript libraries, such as AngularJS. They provide speed and performance benefits, and they can be much more bandwidth-friendly. Google, Microsoft, Yahoo, and other large web organizations offer CDN services for free. You may have noticed that AngularJS provides an option to use the Google CDN as an alternative to downloading the script and hosting it yourself (see the URL in the field labeled CDN).

Browser Support

All modern web browsers support AngularJS. This list includes Safari, Chrome, Firefox, Opera, IE9 and later versions, and mobile browsers, including Android, Chrome Mobile, and iOS Safari. Generally speaking, browser support is not an issue; AngularJS is very much here and now.

■ **Note**   The ninth and later versions of Internet Explorer are supported. At the time I write this, support for Internet Explorer 8 is about to be dropped.

Of course, you should always know your target audience and test your applications across as broad a range of devices and platforms as possible. Fortunately, the AngularJS community is large (and growing fast), so it's definitely worth heading in that direction if you have questions. Of particular interest are the case studies that you can use to get a sense of AngularJS in action (see `http://builtwith.angularjs.org`).

Your First AngularJS Application

Let's start our journey toward AngularJS enlightenment by creating a very small and simple application, albeit one that demonstrates little more than how to include AngularJS on a web page, and use it to display the traditional Hello World greeting.

Save Listing 2-1 into your BeginningAngularJS folder.

Listing 2-1. Hello World

```
<!DOCTYPE html>
<html ng-app>
<head>
  <title>Listing 2-1</title>
  <script src="js/angular.min.js"></script>
</head>
<body>
  <p>Hello {{'Wor' + 'ld'}}</p>
</body>
</html>
```

While this is about as simple as it gets, there is actually quite a lot going on here. It's well worth dissecting this and reviewing how each line works, as there are a few important concepts at play—concepts that are fundamental to the way AngularJS works and, therefore, key to how to think in AngularJS.

■ **Caution**   AngularJS isn't quite like other frameworks, and it may require you to think a little differently than you are used to. I initially found that I was writing AngularJS code with my jQuery hat on, and this proved extremely counterproductive! I will talk more about this shortly in the section "Declarative vs. Procedural Programming."

In the first line of the program, we have the HTML5 doctype. Though this is not strictly necessary for AngularJS to work, it is the doctype you should be using for today's rich Internet applications.

The second line is where it becomes interesting. We have declared an ngApp directive within the opening HTML element. I will expand on this directive (and directives in general) a little bit later in this chapter and then much more in Chapter 5. We use ngApp to let AngularJS know which element is to be considered the root of the application. As we have declared it within the HTML element, we are declaring that the whole document is to be "under the control" of AngularJS.

Moving down to the fifth line, you can see that we have included the AngularJS library using the script element. If we didn't include the AngularJS library, we wouldn't see any AngularJS goodness.

Now for something very exciting: if you move down to the eighth line, you will see an AngularJS expression, as delimited by the opening and closing double curly braces—{{ and }}. We keep things nice and simple here and concatenate the two string literals 'Wor' and 'ld'.

AngularJS expressions are powerful, and you will see many of them in this book. Here we use one in a somewhat contrived way, simply to illustrate how they are put into action. The interpolated value is, of course, the string World.

When we place an expression between double curly braces like this, we create an expression binding. In a nutshell, this means that the value of the expression is bound. Anytime it changes, the binding will update too. Bindings and expressions will be second nature to you in no time, as these are at the core of how AngularJS works.

You can see the result of this in Figure 2-2.

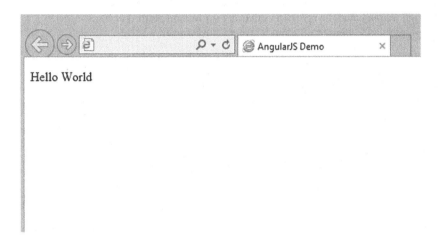

Figure 2-2. *The output of our Hello World listing*

I said it was very exciting, didn't I? Well, perhaps I exaggerated a little bit. Nonetheless, it is an AngularJS application, and it gets you started on your journey. We will do something a little more interesting shortly, but let's summarize the key steps we took in Listing 2-1.

- We used the ngApp directive to inform our page that it should consider itself under the control of AngularJS.

- We then used a script element to include the AngularJS library.

- Just to prove everything was hooked up correctly, we used a simple AngularJS expression binding to do some basic string concatenation.

That wasn't difficult at all, but let's tinker with Listing 2-1 a bit, just to get a little bit more insight into how AngularJS ticks. Listing 2-2 is a revised version.

Listing 2-2. Tinkering with the Hello World Listing

```
<!DOCTYPE html>
<html>
<head>
    <title>Listing 2-2</title>
    <script src="js/angular.min.js"></script>
</head>
<body>
```

```
    <p ng-app>Hello {{'Wor' + 'ld'}}</p>
    <p>Hello {{'Wor' + 'ld'}}</p>
</body>
</html>
```

All that we have done here is to move the ngApp directive out of the opening HTML element and place it on the first paragraph element. We also added another paragraph element, which is almost identical to the first. However this one is without an ngApp directive. Save Listing 2-2, and load it up in your browser.

Two interesting things happen:

1. The first interesting thing is that the expression binding in the first paragraph worked just as it did before. Even though we relocated the ngApp directive, the expression binding is still nested within its boundaries and, therefore, still under AngularJS control.

2. The second interesting thing is that the second paragraph uses an expression too. However, this expression binding simply renders as is; it is not evaluated at all. AngularJS simply isn't interested in it, because it is not contained within the boundaries of an ngApp directive. In fact, AngularJS has no knowledge of this particular paragraph element or anything contained within it.

In this book, I will always declare the ngApp directive on the HTML element. While it is handy to know that you can tell AngularJS to manage only a specific portion of the DOM, I want you to see the effect of it being in the wrong location, or missing altogether. Forgetting to add the ngApp directive is one of the most common mistakes that beginners make.

■ **Note**   It is technically possible, though not terribly common, to use more than one ngApp directive per page. There are a couple of limitations, however. First, they must not be nested within each other. Second, you have to write extra code to make AngularJS recognize all but the first one. It's a relatively advanced scenario that I will not be covering in this book.

This sets us up nicely with some working AngularJS code, but it doesn't really hint much at what makes AngularJS such a powerful framework. Listing 2-3, while still small and simple, starts edging toward this.

Listing 2-3. Live Updates

```
<!DOCTYPE html>
<html ng-app>

<head>
  <title>Listing 2-3</title>
    <script src="js/angular.min.js"></script>
</head>

<body>

  <label>City: </label><input ng-model="city" type="text" /></label>
  <p>You entered: {{city}}</p>

</body>
</html>
```

Here we have declared the expected ngApp directive and AngularJS script reference with which, it is hoped, you are already comfortable. The two important lines are the two lines contained within the body element. The first declares a standard HTML text input, but with one very important addition—the ngModel directive, which we have assigned the value of city. The second line, via an expression binding, uses this value to reference the text that the end user enters into the text field.

Save Listing 2-3 and load it up in your browser. This is where the magic starts to happen. Start typing into the text field and watch as the text in the paragraph below the text field updates in real time. What makes it so magical is the amount of code that it took to achieve this result—not very much code at all, no?

It's not really magic, of course. At least not in the Harry Potter sense. However, something very sophisticated is clearly taking place. Already, we can see that AngularJS must be hard at work for us, monitoring the application for data changes, updating the DOM to show these changes to the end user, and other things that we are yet to encounter. Other frameworks require that you tackle some or all of this work yourself. AngularJS wants you to focus on your primary concern—your application, not its plumbing.

Another interesting point is that we didn't actually write any JavaScript code! You will find that AngularJS has a strong lean toward a declarative, as opposed to a procedural, coding style. Obviously, you have to write JavaScript at some point or other, but AngularJS encourages you to put this in the right parts of your application. As you might expect, a good portion of this book will look at just what constitutes these "right parts."

Declarative vs. Procedural Programming

A classic example of a declarative programming language to which many developers can easily relate is SQL. When you write an SQL query against a database such as MySQL, you don't really do the heavy lifting yourself. Instead, you give rather high-level instructions to the database engine via a relatively simple select statement. You don't worry about how the database engine should pull the data together in the most efficient way, and you don't worry about things such as control flow and looping constructs—you just issue a select statement and expect the database to give you back the data that you want. In a sense, you *declare* what you want, and it does the work for you.

Procedural programming, on the other hand, requires a more detailed and lower-level set of instructions. In the extremely procedural C language, for example, you must take great care to reserve memory, detail the specific instructions you want to be executed, and then worry about freeing up memory, making sure your algorithms perform well and are thoroughly tested, and all sorts of other things.

Declarative programming is much more convenient than procedural programming, because it is often faster and easier. You generally don't have the same kind of granular control that you do with procedural programming, but you often don't need it. In fact, as you will see, AngularJS won't mind at all if you want to adopt a procedural approach when it suits you.

Directives and Expressions

Let's have a look at a few more AngularJS directives. Directives are a great example of the declarative programming style that AngularJS encourages you to adopt. They are also at the heart of AngularJS, and they are a crucial part of how you will deliver a great user experience.

What Is a Directive?

AngularJS uses directives to augment HTML with extra functionality. Essentially, *directives* are a convenient way to declaratively call JavaScript functions. We will look at directives in much more detail in Chapter 5. For now, though, following is a decent overview of directives.

Let's try out the very handy ngShow directive. Check out Listing 2-4.

Listing 2-4. A First Look at ngShow

```
<!DOCTYPE html>
<html ng-app>
<head>
    <title>Listing 2-4</title>
<script src="js/angular.min.js"></script>
</head>
<body>

<p ng-show="true">Paragraph 1, can you see me?</p>
<p ng-show="false">Paragraph 2, can you see me?</p>
<p ng-show="1 == 1">Paragraph 3, can you see me?</p>
<p ng-show="1 == 2">Paragraph 4, can you see me?</p>

</body>
</html>
```

Listing 2-4 shows four paragraph elements, each has been "augmented" by an AngularJS directive that goes by the name of ngShow.

■ **Note**   The astute reader may have noticed that I have used the term ngShow in my writing and the subtly different term ng-show in my code. Which is correct? AngularJS typically refers to directives in documentation by their case-sensitive, CamelCase name (for example, ngShow) but refers to directives in the DOM by using lowercase, dash-delimited attributes (for example, ng-show).

What does ngShow do? Much of the answer is in the name. The ngShow directive will show, or hide, the element on which it is declared, based on the expression provided to it. Load up Listing 2-4 in your browser, and you will see that only the first and third paragraphs appear (as confirmed in Figure 2-3). They only appear because, in both cases, their respective expressions evaluate to the Boolean value of true. The second and fourth paragraphs, however, do not appear because their respective ngShow expressions evaluate to the Boolean value of false.

Figure 2-3. *ngShow in action*

■ **Tip** If an ngShow expression evaluates to false, then a CSS class named `.ng-hide` is dynamically added to the element, causing it to become hidden. So, the element still exists in the DOM, but it is not displayed.

The ngShow directive is very handy. You will use it often for hiding or showing regions of your user interface, based on user input or other conditions.

Another common directive is the ngClick directive. Just like ngShow, ngClick expects an expression, but unlike ngShow, this expression is only evaluated when the element it is declared upon is clicked.

Listing 2-5 shows ngClick in action. Load it up in your browser and press the Increment button a few times.

Listing 2-5. Demonstrating ngClick

```
<!doctype html>
<html  ng-app>
<head>
  <title>Listing 2-5</title>
  <script src="js/angular.min.js"></script>
</head>
<body>
   <button ng-click="count = count + 1" ng-init="count = 0">
   Increment
 </button>
 count: {{count}}
</body>
</html>
```

As you might have guessed, clicking the Increment button causes the value of count to increment. Each time the button is clicked, ngClick evaluates the expression. As the count variable is used in an expression binding, we can see its value updated in real time.

Here we have also used the ngInit directive. You typically won't use ngInit very much, if at all, for reasons that will make more sense when I discuss the MVC (Model View Controller) approach predominantly used in AngularJS applications. However, here we use it to initialize the count variable to 0. You could just as easily have set this value to, say, 10, in order to increment from a starting value of 10 instead of 0.

What Are Expressions?

You've seen a few expressions already, but what exactly are they? Essentially, they are JavaScript expressions, just like the ones you already know and love. However, there are a few important differences.

- In AngularJS, expressions are not evaluated against the global window object; instead, they are evaluated against a scope object.

- You don't get the usual ReferenceError or TypeError when trying to evaluate undefined properties. AngularJS expressions are forgiving in that regard.

- You cannot use conditionals, loops, or exceptions. This is a good thing; you don't want complex logic inside expressions. (In Chapter 3, I will discuss where you do want them.)

- You can use AngularJS filters to format data before displaying it. (I cover Filters in Chapter 4.)

To get a sense of how expressions work and what you can do with them, take a look at Listing 2-6.

Listing 2-6. A Quick Look at AngularJS Expressions

```
<!DOCTYPE html>
<html ng-app>
<head>
<title>Listing 2-5</title>
  <script src="js/angular.min.js"></script>
</head>
<body>

  <h1>Expression Samples</h1>

  <!-- Basic arithmetic -->
  <p>6 + 4 = {{6 + 4}}</p>

  <!-- Using a JavaScript string method -->
  <p>{{"Beginning AngularJS".toUpperCase()}}</p>

  <!-- Searching for an occurence of 'D' -->
  <p>{{"ABCDEFG".indexOf('D')}}</p>

  <!-- Ternary operation -->
  <p>{{1==1 ? "Red" : "Blue"}}</p>

</body>
</html>
```

There is nothing complex going on here. It's all run-of-the-mill JavaScript code but now using AngularJS expressions. Figure 2-4 shows the results.

Expression Samples

6 + 4 = 10

BEGINNING ANGULARJS

3

Red

Figure 2-4. *AngularJS expressions in action*

There are definitely a few more things to know about expressions, and we will get to them as you learn more about how we should be structuring and organizing our code. This is exactly what I will discuss in the next chapter.

Summary

This chapter explored the concept of frameworks and why you would want to use one. At this stage, I hope that you are feeling quite confident that AngularJS is the right one for you and that you are eager to learn much more in the coming chapters.

You have downloaded and installed AngularJS, gained a sense of its "declarative-powered" directives, and witnessed its very tidy use of expressions. You are in great shape already, and it's nearly time to get into the finer details. Before we do that, however, I will take a slight detour in Chapter 3 and discuss some big picture topics, including how to organize and structure AngularJS applications.

CHAPTER 3

Introduction to MVC

We have taken a quick look at AngularJS and how to get a simple Angular-based web page up and running, but the reality is that you don't need AngularJS if all you want to do is build a very basic application.

One of the major strengths of AngularJS lies in its ability to help you properly organize and structure your applications, and very small applications tend not to benefit much at all from this. Of course, smaller applications should be properly structured too, but such applications are not as likely to require the rigid underpinnings and formal structure of a medium- or large-sized application. The way you would approach pitching a tent is not the same way you would approach building a log cabin.

With that in mind, in this chapter, we will look at what it means to organize and structure an application and how the Model View Controller (MVC) pattern can help you to do both.

Design Patterns

Before we get into MVC, let's talk about design patterns for a moment. After all, MVC is a design pattern, so it would be good to know what design patterns are and why you should care about them. Essentially, a *design pattern* is a documented solution to a recurring problem that programmers have identified—usually in a particular context. Design patterns won't give you the code you need to solve a given problem, but they will propose a well-thought-out and generally accepted approach that you might want to consider adopting yourself.

A good way to think of design patterns is that they are like recipes that have been created by programmers who have spent a lot of time in the trenches. These programmers have found out, often through a combination of talent and old-fashioned trial and error, a lot of really great ways to solve specific kinds of problems. Furthermore, these programmers have decided to share these recipes with everyone else.

There isn't really a formal standard that states how design pattern documentation should be written, but we will examine something fairly typical. You will generally find something along the lines of what I have outlined in Table 3-1 on design pattern documentation.

Table 3-1. *Typical Design Pattern Documentation*

Title	Description
Pattern Name and Classification	A name that helps in referring to the pattern, often with a classification stating the type of pattern it is
Intent	The goal of the pattern and the reason it exists
Motivation	A scenario consisting of a problem and a context in which this pattern can be used
Collaboration	A description of how classes and objects used in the pattern interact
Sample Code	Actual code showing how the pattern can be used in a programming language

Sometimes, you will find a lot more information about a design pattern than what I present here, but usually you will find at least this much to help you understand its purpose and its intended uses.

■ **Tip**   There is a school of thought that says that MVC is not a design pattern at all, rather it's an an architectural pattern. There is no right or wrong answer, in my opinion, and the important word here is *pattern*.

After reading through any given design pattern documentation and looking at any associated diagrams (which are usually UML based; see the Tip here), you are typically in a much better position to determine if it is applicable to the particular problem you are trying to solve. Patterns certainly are a tremendously useful resource, but there is one really important thing to understand about them up front: they are not silver bullets. Think of them more like friends that give good advice and not so much like divine intervention when you can't find an answer.

■ **Tip**   The Unified Modeling Language (UML) is a general-purpose modeling language used in software development. It provides a standard way to visualize the design of software systems.

Let's study a very common and relatively straightforward design pattern called the Singleton pattern. This one is well worth knowing as an AngularJS developer, though I have chosen it mainly because it is more digestible in this introductory book than other, more involved design patterns. I don't want to scare you off quite so early in the book! Read through the sample Singleton pattern documentation in Table 3-2.

Table 3-2. *Singleton Design Pattern Documentation*

Title	Description
Pattern Name and Classification	Singleton: an object creational pattern
Intent	Ensures that a class has only one instance and provides a global point of access to it
Motivation	Sometimes it makes sense to control the creation of certain objects. For example, rather than allow an application to create numerous database connection objects, it may make more sense to allow for a single connection object, which an application can access through a gateway object, that provides access to a single instance.
Collaboration	The Singleton collaborates with external objects.
Implementation	Creates a class that can create a single instance of itself. This should be the only way an instance can be created.
Sample Code	Sample code is shown in Listing 3-1.

Let's work through a scenario. Assume that we found this design pattern documentation through an online search after recognizing an issue within our application. Far too many objects of the same type were being created. Let's further assume that these objects were quite expensive to create, with each object's initialization causing time-consuming and bandwidth-intensive connections to a remote system. We need to fix this.

■ **Note**   One of the first and most well received books on design patterns is *Design Patterns: Elements of Reusable Object-Oriented Software* by Erich Gamma et al. (Addison-Wesley Professional, 2015). It's well worth checking this book out, if you want to learn more about design patterns and how to use them.

So, we have read through the patterns documentation, and we want to figure out if and how this particular pattern can be of any use. The Motivation section of Table 3-2 has got our attention—it certainly seems to fit the bill. It's definitely worth further study to see if the code sample that came with it can shed any light on how we could put it into practice.

Let's look at the sample code in Listing 3-1. Don't worry too much if you don't fully grasp what each and every line is doing, as this listing uses some advanced JavaScript techniques that you may not be familiar with yet. Nonetheless, do pay special attention to the comments.

Listing 3-1. A JavaScript Implementation of the Singleton Pattern

```
var Logger = (function() {

  // private variable to hold the only
  // instance of Logger that will exist
  var loggerInstance;

  // Create the logger instance
  var createLogger = function() {
    var _logWarning = function(message) {
      // some complex work coud go here, but
      // let's just fake it
```

```
      return message.toUpperCase();
    };

    return {
      logWarning: _logWarning
    };

  };

  return {

    // Here is the crucial part. First we check
    // to see if an instance already exists. If
    // it does, we return it. If it does not, we
    // create it.

    getInstance: function() {
      if (!loggerInstance) {
        loggerInstance = createLogger();
      }
      return loggerInstance;
    }

  };
})();

// Notice how we use getInstance() and we
// do not use direct object creation with the
// new keyword

var myLogger = Logger.getInstance();
myLogger.logWarning("Memory use nearing maximum!");
```

This code sample represents a typical code snippet that you might find accompanying design pattern documentation. It just so happens to be written in JavaScript, but it could just as easily have been written in C#, Java, or any other language. (In fact, that is more likely to be the case.)

The essential aspect of Listing 3-1 is that it privately manages a single instance of a logger object. It isn't possible to create a new logger object directly. We have to use the getInstance function to access the already-existing logger object (or, if it didn't exist already, the newly created logger object). This is the essence of the pattern, and it seems to be a good solution for the problem we face in our own scenario: our applications issue of numerous objects of the same type being needlessly created, over and over.

Along with a code sample such as this, you are likely to come across a UML diagram showing how objects used in a pattern relate and interact with one another. I will stop short of getting into the nuances of UML, and in the case of the Singleton pattern, by definition, there aren't that many relations and interactions to show.

The usefulness of design patterns can be difficult to overstate. In our scenario, we had a serious problem within our application, and the Singleton design pattern turned out to be a good way to solve it. This is a relatively simple example of using design patterns to find solutions about which we can feel confident. Other programmers have used this approach, and it is one that has come about through collaboration, testing, refinement, and lots of real-world use. That has to be a good thing.

Design patterns are indeed a valuable resource, but you still have to put plenty of thought into how (and whether or not) to use any given design pattern in a particular context. As specific as design patterns may seem in their description and usage, they are still generalized solutions that may or may not apply to your needs. That being said, a well-documented design pattern will help you make these decisions.

■ **Tip**   Reading up on design patterns is actually a great way to improve your code. You may have solved a problem in a particular way, only to find that there is a design pattern dedicated to avoiding the approach you took! It might not be good for the ego, but it's a great way to learn.

With this short introduction to design patterns now complete, we can look at the specific pattern that we will use throughout the rest of this book: the Model View Controller (MVC) pattern. You have to learn what MVC is, so that you can apply it within AngularJS. However, we don't actually have to write our own MVC solution, because AngularJS has what you need baked right into the framework.

Model View Controller

I hope our quick discussion about design patterns has brought to the front of your mind that there are good ways and not so good ways to design your applications and that there are helpful recipes out there that can help you design better applications. Fortunately, the folks who created AngularJS have already put all of the pieces of the MVC pattern into place for you. As the MVC pattern is an architectural pattern, which is realized through a number of other design patterns, I won't include the rather extensive documentation for it here. Instead, we will focus on the AngularJS implementation of it and consider what it does for us.

Let's talk about the three major parts of the MVC pattern: the model, the view, and the controller. We're not really speaking at a code level here; rather, we are talking at a higher level about how to organize and structure your applications. MVC is often considered an architectural pattern, which is essentially a pattern that addresses some aspect of an application's overall organization and structure.

We will see how MVC comes together in code form later in this chapter, so don't worry too much if it all seems a little abstract as I am discussing it.

■ **Tip**   Architectural patterns are often realized through a number of design patterns. As I said earlier, however, the keyword here is *pattern*. It really depends on what level you happen to be speaking (and quite possibly to whom you happen to be talking).

Model

The *model* represents the underlying, logical structure of data in a software application. It's a common mistake to think of the model as the database behind your application, and it is much better to view the model as the body of code that represents the data.

View

A *view* is the body of code that represents the user interface (all of the things that the user can see and to which the user can respond on the screen, such as buttons, dialog boxes, and so on). An application generally has multiple views, and each view often represents some portion of your model.

Controller

You can think of the *controller* as the *intermediary* for the view and the model. Examine Figure 3-1. You can see that the lines of communication correspond to this idea.

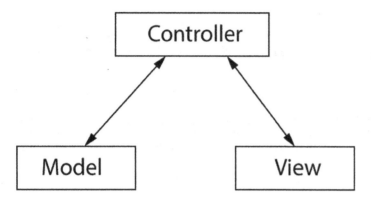

Figure 3-1. *The MVC lines of communication*

A Separation of Concerns

Great! We have some background on the three core components of MVC and how they relate to one another. Though, at this stage, it may not be entirely clear why we should be using it. Now let's take a look at the underlying purpose of this pattern and what sort of problems it solves.

As is clear from the definitions above, the controller is actually keeping the model and the view separated—one has no direct knowledge of the other. This is a fairly common design in software engineering, and the term used to describe it is *decoupling*.

When you organize your applications in this manner, it promotes a principle known as Separation of Concerns. Software that has been built around this principle tends to have distinct parts, each of which looks after a particular concern. MVC is a great way of achieving this Separation of Concerns, and before I end this chapter, we will take a quick first look at how AngularJS helps you build your applications in this manner.

I have talked a little bit about MVC and Separation of Concerns, but how do these ideas translate into benefits for programmers and end users? Why should we take the extra time and effort it takes to build our applications in this manner?

Why MVC Matters

A classic benefit of MVC is that you can, with relative ease, add a new format to your application. That is, you can start off with a standard HTML-based set of views and then later add a new set of views supporting a totally different format, such as Silverlight or a native mobile front end. Trying to achieve something like this when your application has been poorly designed would be a nightmare. Take it from someone who has tried it both with and without an MVC-style architecture—the difference in the effort required is huge!

The benefit stated previously exists because, through MVC, we apply the principle of Separation of Concerns. The view is in no way exclusively tied to the model, so it is far easier to treat it as a distinct component that we can swap out for another (or, as is quite common, compliment with another).

There are also benefits with regard to the methodologies and processes you (and your team) can use. For example, Test-Driven Development (TDD) is very popular at present, and it leads to applications that are much easier to test and continue to test as the application matures. Without achieving a solid Separation of Concerns, it can become much trickier to set up good tests.

There really are many reasons to use MVC, and most of them are based around the commonsense idea that it leads to a much more organized and well-structured application, one with distinct roles and responsibilities. This might seem great from the point of view of the programmer who has to build and maintain the application—clearly life is going to be much easier for this programmer if code has been carefully crafted and well-structured—but how is this of any benefit to the end user of the application?

End users benefit from MVC because it leads to applications that are far less prone to bugs and much easier to maintain. This is, of course, a huge benefit, and perhaps the single most important thing toward which we strive. An end user who is provided with stable software, and who is given future releases and updates that don't break things, is a happy end user!

MVC is a tried and tested way to build robust applications. Despite the extra up-front effort, it can save hours and hours of time later on. As I said earlier, don't worry if this all seems a little abstract at this stage, because once you see it in action, it will all click into place. Before you know it, it will feel like second nature to you.

MVC the AngularJS Way

Let's put the theory into practice—at least just a little bit, as this section will not be much more than a drive-by look at the topics that I will cover in much more detail throughout the rest of this book.

AngularJS makes the creation of MVC-style applications relatively straightforward and, in my opinion, quite enjoyable. I will point out at this stage, however, that there are a few more moving parts than you may be used to, and a couple of new concepts that you will need to wrap your head around.

Let's kick things off by looking at how the model, view, and controller manifest themselves in actual code, via a very simple code example. I will use a partial code listing to represent each concern, and then I will pull it all together into a complete code listing. This way, we can isolate the important parts first and then look at them working together as a whole. The code shown in Listing 3-1 is what we will use to represent our model.

```
var employees = ['Christopher Grant', 'Monica Grant', 'Christopher Grant', 'Jennifer Grant'];
```

The `employees` variable is simply a hard-coded array of employee names. In the real world, this array would usually be populated from a data store of some kind–an SQL database, for example. We don't need to complicate the listing with data-access code. (I will, however, discuss AngularJS support for accessing data later in the book.) The important thing to understand about this line of code is that the array of employees is what represents our model.

It's worth making a clarification here, as there is often confusion around the term *model*. Is the model all of the objects that represent the entities in our data store, or is it just the one specific piece of information that we use in a view (employees being an example of the latter)? The short and simple answer is that it depends on the context, although it is quite common to refer to the former as the *domain model* and the latter as the *view model*.

Let's turn our attention to the view. Here is a very simple example of what an AngularJS view looks like. In AngularJS parlance, we would call this a *view template*. As was discussed earlier, the view is concerned with presentation. More often than not, it represents the presentation of data from our model.

```
Number of Employees: {{ ourEmployees.length}}</h2>
```

This is basically just HTML and an AngularJS expression, and I will cover what's happening here in a moment. Right now, however, I want you to notice something interesting about Listing 3-2 and Listing 3-3. Neither has any dependency on the other. This is good, and it is in line with our discussions around the desire to achieve a Separation of Concerns. Though it does raise a very interesting question: How does the model data, that is, the employees array, find its way into the view? Let's investigate this right now.

Listing 3-2 is where the really interesting stuff starts to happen, as the AngularJS MVC framework is starting to emerge. The function `MyFirstCtrl` is the controller. It is a common convention in AngularJS to use Pascal case when naming the controller function (that is, to start with a capital letter and use a capital letter for each new word).

Listing 3-2. MVC in Action

```
function MyFirstCtrl($scope) {

// populate the employees variable with some model data
var employees = ['Christopher Grant', 'Monica Grant', 'Christopher Grant', 'Jennifer
Grant'];

// Now put this model data into the scope so it can be used in the view
    $scope.ourEmployees = employees;
  }
```

Review Listing 3-2. We assign the model data to the ourEmployees property that we set on this $scope object. This is the answer: this is how the model data, the employees array, finds its way into the view. The $scope object was supplied to our controller function by the AngularJS framework, and all that we needed to do was to populate it with the data that we wanted to make available to the view.

Glance back at the view in Listing 3-2, and notice that the expression uses a reference to ourEmployees. You can think of this expression {{ourEmployees.length}} as effectively being the same thing as {{$scope.ourEmployees. length}}. Don't actually use a scope reference in this manner within an expression; it won't work, as the use of the current scope object is implicit.

Listing 3-3 pulls all of this together into a single MVC example. It's short and simple, but the essence of AngularJS is on display here.

Listing 3-3. A Complete MVC Example

```
<!DOCTYPE html>
<html ng-app>

<head>
  <script src="js/angular.min.js"></script>
  <script>

    function MyFirstCtrl($scope) {

      var employees = ['Catherine Grant', 'Monica Grant',
        'Christopher Grant', 'Jennifer Grant'
      ];

      $scope.ourEmployees = employees;
    }

  </script>
</head>

<body ng-controller='MyFirstCtrl'>

  <h2>Number of Employees: {{ ourEmployees.length}}</h2>

</body>
</html>
```

The output, as shown in Figure 3-2, is simply a count of the number of employees, courtesy of the `Array.length` property.

Number of Employees: 4

Figure 3-2. *Counting the number of employees (output of Listing 3-3)*

Perhaps the most important aspect of Listing 3-3 is how we use a scope object, an instance of which, as we discussed, was passed into our controller function by the framework. It really is quite fundamental to how AngularJS does much of its work. We can already see it being used to decouple the model from the view, but it actually does something a little bit more impressive than keep our code clean and modular. It is also a key player in the framework's ability to keep the model and the view in sync with each other. The changes made to the model were immediately reflected in the view; we did not have to do any Document Object Model (DOM) manipulation.

■ **Tip** If you have been working with jQuery for a while, you might find the lack of DOM manipulation a bit peculiar at first. jQuery is all about DOM manipulation, and you might have to make an effort to shake off that way of thinking when you are working with AngularJS.

We are nearly at the end of this chapter, but before moving on, I want to show you one more code sample. Listing 3-4 demonstrates another AngularJS approach toward code organization, to keep things clean and crisp.

Listing 3-4. Displaying the Employee Names

```
<!DOCTYPE html>
<html ng-app>

<head>
  <script src="js/angular.min.js"></script>
  <script>

    function MyFirstCtrl($scope) {

      var employees = ['Catherine Grant', 'Monica Grant',
        'Christopher Grant', 'Jennifer Grant'
      ];

      $scope.ourEmployees = employees;
    }

  </script>
</head>
```

```
<body ng-controller='MyFirstCtrl'>

  <h2>Number of Employees: {{ ourEmployees.length}}</h2>
  <p ng-repeat="employee in ourEmployees">{{employee}}</p>

</body>
</html>
```

This listing isn't terribly different from Listing 3-3—there is just one additional line of code. Instead of displaying only the number of employees who work for us, we now use the ngRepeat directive to display the name of each employee who works for us.

The ngRepeat directive will repeat the instance of the element upon which it is declared (a paragraph element in this case) for each item in a collection. As Figure 3-3 shows, this results in a total of four paragraphs: one for each of the employees in the ourEmployees array. Consider this a teaser. ngRepeat is quite powerful, and you will definitely be seeing more of it in coming chapters.

Number of Employees: 4

Catherine Grant

Monica Grant

Christopher Grant

Jennifer Grant

Figure 3-3. *Introducing ngDirective*

Summary

I hope this chapter has started you thinking about the structure and organization of your applications. In the not-so-distant past, a less formal approach to JavaScript development seemed to work well enough. Scripts were small and played only a small role in application development, so it just didn't matter to the extent that it does now.

I started off with a quick discussion about design patterns—just enough to put them on your radar and to let you know that you are not alone. We then looked at the Model View Controller (MVC) pattern, the pattern predominantly used when building AngularJS applications.

A quick look at ngRepeat demonstrated that AngularJS isn't just helping us with the higher-level structural aspects of our applications. The declarative approach taken with directives also helps us to keep our code clear and concise.

JavaScript is used to build significant portions of web applications, so it is always important to consider application design and structure.

CHAPTER 4

■ ■ ■

Filters and Modules

When working with data that has been retrieved from a database, you will spend a lot of time working with raw unformatted data. It's not at all uncommon to come across dates that are formatted unusually, numbers that have far too many digits after the decimal point, and people's names that are in all uppercase letters. Keep in mind that data is not always stored in the best format for our own applications, and its original purpose might have been to service a totally different kind of application. When presenting data to end users, however, we need a way to deal with such things. Angular JS filters are often a very good way to do just that.

In this chapter, we will look at AngularJS filters, both the built-in variety and custom filters. We will also look at AngularJS modules, which are important in their own right and are a prerequisite for creating custom filters.

Introduction to Filters

AngularJS filters format the value of an expression for display to the end user. They don't actually change the underlying data, but they do change how it is displayed in the particular case in which the filter is applied.

This is much easier to understand with the help of an example. First, let's start off with some sample data (see Listing 4-1) to which we can apply some filters.

Listing 4-1. Raw Sample Data

```
<script>
    function MyFilterDemoCtrl($scope) {

        var someData = {
            firstName: 'JENNA',
            surname: 'GRANT',
            dateJoined: new Date(2010, 2, 23),
            consumption: 123.659855,
            plan: 'super-basic-plan'
        };

        $scope.data = someData;


    }
</script>
```

Data like this would typically come back from a request to a web service or a database, but we only want some sample data, so that we can learn about AngularJS filters without the additional distraction of data access code. This fictitious data, captured in a JavaScript object we have named someData in Listing 4-1, represents some customer details. We will use this data as the chapter progresses, starting now with a first look at the AngularJS filter syntax.

The first filter we will look at will address the issue of the firstName and surname appearing in uppercase. To improve this slightly, we will change it to lowercase. To achieve this, the main thing to know is that you use the | (pipe) character, to invoke a filter. Later in this chapter, we will look at how to improve upon this even further, by leaving the first character in uppercase and converting only the remaining characters to lowercase, a technique known as *title casing*.

Listing 4-2 shows how this is done. The MyFilterDemoCtrl controller's only task here is to make the data available to the view. As you will recall from the last chapter, placing it in the scope does this.

Listing 4-2. Angular Filter Example

```html
<!DOCTYPE html>
<html>
<head>
    <title>Listing 4-2</title>
    <script src="js/angular.min.js"></script>
    <script>
        function MyFilterDemoCtrl($scope) {

            var someData = {
                firstName: 'JENNA',
                surname: 'GRANT',
                dateJoined: new Date(2010, 2, 23),
                consumption: 123.659855,
                plan: 'super-basic-plan'
            };

            $scope.data = someData;


        }
    </script>

</head>
<body ng-app ng-controller="MyFilterDemoCtrl">

<p>
    <!-- Unfiltered data -->
    <strong>First Name</strong>: {{data.firstName}}<br/>
    <strong>Surname:</strong> {{data.surname}}
</p>

<p>
    <!-- Filtered data -->
    <strong>First Name</strong>: {{data.firstName | lowercase}}<br/>
    <strong>Surname:</strong> {{data.surname | lowercase }}
</p>


</body>
</html>
```

Listing 4-2 shows how easy it is to apply the lowercase filter. We apply it by stating the value we want to filter, followed by the | (pipe) character and then the name of the filter. The most important aspects of the code are shown in bold. As Figure 4-1 shows, the first paragraph displays the plain unfiltered data, and the second paragraph displays the filtered data.

First Name: JENNA
Surname: GRANT

First Name: jenna
Surname: grant

Figure 4-1. *lowercase filter—before and after*

You won't be very surprised to learn that there is a built-in filter named uppercase, which, unsurprisingly, converts characters to uppercase. AngularJS ships with a set of other handy filters, and we look at these in the next section. However, before we get to them, let's take a step back and consider why we might want to use filters. After all, JavaScript already has what you need to perform these kinds of tasks. For example, we could just as easily have added the code for lowercasing data values directly to the controller, instead of using filters. Listing 4-3 takes this approach, and it produces the very same result as Listing 4-2.

Listing 4-3. Achieving Same Result Without Filter

```
<script>
    function MyFilterDemoCtrl($scope) {

        var someData = {
            firstName: 'JENNA',
            surname: 'GRANT',
            dateJoined: new Date(2010, 2, 23),
            consumption: 123.659855,
            plan: 'super-basic-plan'
        };

        // do the lowercaing here instead of using a filter
        someData.firstName = someData.firstName.toLowerCase();
        someData.surname = someData.surname.toLowerCase();
        $scope.data = someData;

    }
</script>
```

Using the approach taken in Listing 4-3, it is true that we bypass the need for filters, but there are a few things to consider before you choose to adopt this approach. As I discussed in the last chapter, one very good reason to use AngularJS is because you want to organize your code better and follow some common software development best practices.

We have talked about the Separation of Concerns principle, so let us take a moment to consider whether or not formatting tasks, such as changing the case of the text we present to our end users, logically belongs in a controller. Doesn't this seem like a task for which the view should be responsible? In one sense, formatting data for presentation is indeed a view-related concern. However, you could also argue that a controller should bear some responsibility for making sure that data is ready for use in the view.

The developers of AngularJS take a stance on this and say that such concerns are better dealt with as the data flows from the controller into the view. In fact, this is why a filter is called a filter; the data is "filtered" as it travels from the controller into the view.

Some filters can be much more complex than simple case converters. In the lowercase scenario, we were able to use a single JavaScript method call directly in the controller without things looking messy and out of place, but had we wanted to implement title casing (whereby the first letter of each word is in uppercase and the remainder are in lowercase), things would have gotten a lot more involved and required a much more modular solution. Obviously, having to repeat such logic in each controller or application in which you might need it is not a very DRY approach.

■ **Tip** The DRY principle states that *"Every piece of knowledge must have a single, unambiguous, and authoritative representation within a system."* An easier way to say this is simply *"Don't Repeat Yourself."*

While it is true that the filter may be added to the view in multiple places, the underlying implementation of that filter need only be written once.

Of course, it is up to you to decide how to approach any given situation. Filters are simply an option that you have at your disposal. Nonetheless, filters are a great way to keep your code modular and clean, as they make for a good unit of reuse across AngularJS projects. In fact, as there is a vibrant developer community both contributing to and sharing AngularJS filters online. They make for a good unit of reuse for everyone.

■ **Tip** A great source of modules (filters, directives, and services) is available at `http://ngmodules.org/`.

Built-in Filters

The empowering aspect of filters is, in my opinion, the ability to create your own filters and share them with the rest of the team (or AngularJS community). That being said, AngularJS ships with a very handy set of filters. We will look at these built-in filters now, starting with the number filter. We will look at how to craft a custom filter before the end of this chapter.

The Number Filter

This filter will help us address another issue with our sample data: the overly precise value of the consumption property (which represents the amount of data that the customer has used for this billing period). Let's make this friendlier by rounding the number of places after the decimal point. Listing 4-4 shows how you can achieve this.

Listing 4-4. Rounding Up Values with the Number Filter

```
<!DOCTYPE html>
<html>
<head>
    <title>Listing 4-4</title>
    <script src="js/angular.min.js"></script>
    <script>
        function MyFilterDemoCtrl($scope) {

            var someData = {
                firstName: 'JENNA',
                surname: 'GRANT',
                dateJoined: new Date(2010, 2, 23),
                consumption: 123.659855,
                plan: 'super-basic-plan'
            };

            $scope.data = someData;

        }
    </script>

</head>
<body ng-controller="MyFilterDemoCtrl">

<p>
    Consumption: {{data.consumption }}<br/>
    Consumption: {{data.consumption | number }}
</p>

</body>
</html>
```

Figure 4-2 shows both the unfiltered and filtered data generated within the paragraph element. This is a slight improvement, as now we have just three digits after the decimal point, instead of six.

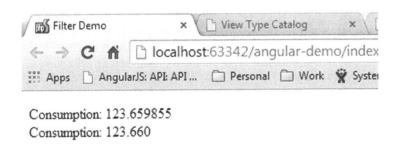

Figure 4-2. *Rounding up numbers with the number filter*

Of course, two digits would be far better and much more in line with end users' expectations. As it happens, the number filter takes a single parameter, which lets you tell it how many decimal places to round a number to. This raises a question: How do you pass parameters to a filter? Fortunately, it is very easy. You use a colon and then enter the parameter value, as shown in the code snippet below.

```
<p>Data used this quarter:<strong> {{ data.consumption | number:2 }} </strong>gigabytes</p>
```

If you replace the paragraph in Listing 4-4 with the preceding snippet and load it into your browser, you will see output identical to that in Figure 4-3.

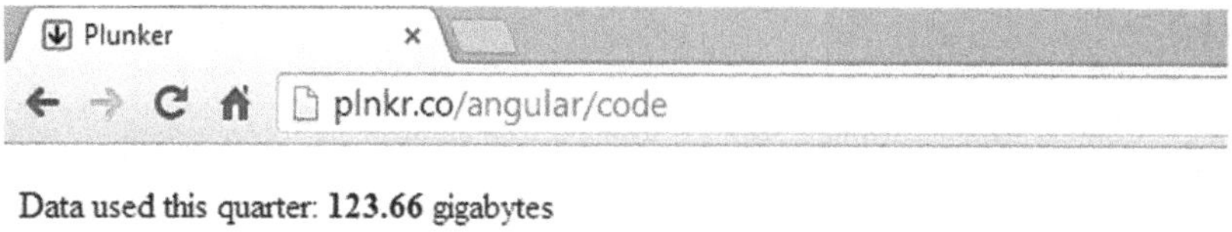

Data used this quarter: **123.66** gigabytes

Figure 4-3. *Using parameters to control the behavior of a filter*

As you can see, the number filter, indeed all filters, are quite easy to use. You can very easily change the format of data without actually changing the underlying data source and without cluttering up the view or controller with presentation-related code.

If you are working with data in which pinpoint accuracy is required, you should be very careful when you are performing rounding operations. Due to the way in which computers represent numbers internally, results are not always totally accurate. A discussion of floating-point-number precision is a little out of scope here, but you can use your favorite search engine to learn more, if this is something that might be important to you.

The Date Filter

The date filter is indispensable and extremely flexible. Consider the `dateJoined` property of our sample data. It has a value which, depending on the time when you view it, looks something like this: `2010-03-22T13:00:00.000Z`. You certainly don't want to be showing it to end users in this format!

■ **Tip**   Don't be fooled by the name. The date filter not only works with dates but also with times.

The date filter's flexibility is due, in part, to the large number of format parameters you can pass to it and how these can be combined to arrive at nearly unlimited ways of displaying dates and times (or portions of dates and times). Table 4-1 and Table 4-2 show the available parameters. Look over these parameters, and then we will review a code listing that shows some of the commonly used ones in action.

Table 4-1. *Date Filter Parameters*

Parameter	Description
yyyy	Four-digit representation of year (for example, AD 1 => 0001, AD 2010 => 2010)
yy	Two-digit representation of year, padded (00–99) (for example, AD 2001 => 01, AD 2010 => 10)
y	One-digit representation of year (for example, AD 1 => 1, AD 199 => 199)
MMMM	Month in year (January-December)
MMM	Month in year (Jan-Dec)
MM	Month in year, padded (01-12)
M	Month in year (1-12)
dd	Day in month, padded (01-31)
d	Day in month (1-31)
EEEE	Day in week (Sunday-Saturday)
EEE	Day in week (Sun-Sat)
HH	Hour in day, padded (00-23)
H	Hour in day (0-23)
hh	Hour in AM/PM, padded (01-12)
h	Hour in AM/PM, (1-12)
mm	Minute in hour, padded (00-59)
m	Minute in hour (0-59)
ss	Second in minute, padded (00-59)
s	Second in minute (0-59)
.sss or ,sss	Millisecond in second, padded (000-999)
a	AM/PM marker
Z	Four-digit (+sign) representation of the time zone offset (-1200 – +1200)
ww	ISO 8601 week of year (00-53)
w	ISO 8601 week of year (0-53)

Table 4-2. *Predefined Date Paramters*

Parameter	Description
medium	equivalent to 'MMM d, y h:mm:ss a' for en_US locale (for example, Sep 3, 2010 12:05:08 PM)
short	equivalent to 'M/d/yy h:mm a' for en_US locale (for example, 9/3/10 12:05PM)
fullDate	equivalent to 'EEEE, MMMM d, y' for en_US locale (for example, Friday, September 3, 2010)
longDate	equivalent to 'MMMM d, y' for en_US locale (for example, September 3, 2010)
mediumDate	equivalent to 'MMM d, y' for en_US locale (for example, Sep 3, 2010)
shortDate	equivalent to 'M/d/yy' for en_US locale (for example, 9/3/10)
mediumTime	equivalent to 'h:mm:ss a' for en_US locale (for example, 12:05:08 PM)
shortTime	equivalent to 'h:mm a' for en_US locale (for example, 12:05 PM)

The parameters in Table 4-1 certainly provide the ability to mix and match and create nearly any date and time structure you need, but more often than not, you only need a typical date representation. For this, you can make use of the predefined parameters described in Table 4-2.

I won't cover all possible date parameter combinations—that would make for an extremely long code listing! Listing 4-5, however, does show some typical date filter usage. The examples that are output in the first three paragraph elements make use of the predefined parameters, and the example that is output in the last paragraph element shows the "mix and match" approach.

Listing 4-5. The Date Filter in Action

```
<!DOCTYPE html>
<html>
<head>
    <title>Listing 4-5</title>
    <script src="js/angular.min.js"></script>
    <script>
        function MyFilterDemoCtrl($scope) {

            var someData = {
                firstName: 'JENNA',
                surname: 'GRANT',
                dateJoined: new Date(2010, 2, 23),
                consumption: 123.659855,
                plan: 'super-basic-plan'
            };

            $scope.data = someData;

        }
    </script>

</head>
<body ng-app ng-controller="MyFilterDemoCtrl">
```

```
<p>medium:<strong> {{ data.dateJoined | date:'medium'}} </strong></p>

<p>mediumDate:<strong> {{ data.dateJoined | date:'mediumDate'}} </strong></p>

<p>shortDate:<strong> {{ data.dateJoined | date:'shortDate'}} </strong></p>

<p>This customer joined in the month of {{ data.dateJoined | date:'MMMM'}} on a {{
data.dateJoined | date:'EEEE'}} at {{ data.dateJoined | date:'ha'}}</p>

</body>
</html>
```

In most cases, the predefined date parameters more than fit the bill; though the last paragraph shows that you can also take a more granular approach. You can see the results in Figure 4-4.

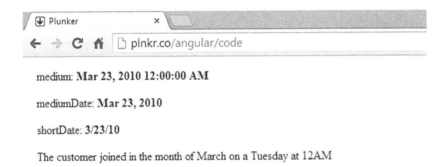

Figure 4-4. *Date filter parameters in action*

Notice that to produce the month and the day, we use 'MMMM' and 'EEEE', respectively, which both appear in Table 4-1. You will not, however, see 'ha', as used to produce the time portion (12AM) in Table 4-1. You will see an 'h' and an 'a', the former being the hour, and the latter being the AM/PM marker. It is perfectly acceptable, and often necessary, to combine date parameters in this manner.

The *limitTo* Filter

We will finish up on the built-in filters with a look at the limitTo filter. This handy filter lets you limit the amount of information displayed from an array. It does this by creating a new array, which contains a subset of the items that are contained in the original array. To showcase the usefulness of this filter, we will add a new property to our sample data source. This new property will contain the customer's historical data usage for the last 12 months. Listing 4-6 is the controller, revised to show this new property.

Listing 4-6. Adding Historical Data to the Data Source

```
<script>
    function MyFilterDemoCtrl($scope) {

        var someData = {
            firstName: 'JENNA',
            surname: 'GRANT',
            dateJoined: new Date(2010, 2, 23),
            consumption: 123.659855,
            plan: 'super-basic-plan',

            // Last 12 months of data usage
                monthlyUsageHistory:
                [123.659855,
                89.645222,
                97.235644,
                129.555555,
                188.699855,
                65.652545,
                123.659855,
                89.645222,
                97.235644,
                129.555555,
                188.699855,
                65.652545]
        };

        $scope.data = someData;

    }
</script>
```

We have 12 months of data in the `monthlyUsageHistory` array, but this could just as easily be, say, five years' worth of data. Listing 4-7 uses the `limitTo` filter to display a summary view of the data (only the last three values).

Listing 4-7. Displaying a Subset of the `monthlyUsageHistory` Data

```
<body ng-app ng-controller="MyFilterDemoCtrl">

<h2>Gigabytes used over the last 3 months</h2>
<ul>
    <li ng-repeat="gigabytes in data.monthlyUsageHistory | limitTo:5">
        {{ gigabytes | number:2}}
    </li>
</ul>

</body>
```

Using ngRepeat, we loop through the monthlyUsageHistory array and output each value (which itself is formatted using the number filter). As Figure 4-5 shows, only the first five items are displayed. This is because we did not, in fact, loop through the monthlyUsageHistory array. What we actually did was loop through a totally new array; an array which was produced by the limitTo filter.

Figure 4-5. *Using the limitTo filter to display a subset of data*

Of course, if you wanted to show only the first three items, you could do so by using limitTo:3. What if you wanted to show only the last three items? Specifying a negative value can do this. If you replace the li element in Listing 4-7 so that it uses the following code snippet, you should see results like those shown in Figure 4-6.

```
<li ng-repeat="gb in data.monthlyUsageHistory | limitTo:-3">
```

Figure 4-6. *Using limitTo to show items from the end of an array*

■ **Tip** Filters do not change the underlying data upon which they operate.

There are other handy built-in filters that you can use, and you can find these in the API documentation at https://docs.angularjs.org/api/ng/filter. We will take a quick time-out from filters now and look at Angular modules. An understanding of modules will put us in a much better position to tackle custom filters; which we will do in the last section of this chapter.

AngularJS Modules

So far, we have not looked at AngularJS modules. Instead, we have placed all of our code within a controller embedded within our HTML file, using the script tag. This approach has its place, but it is usually confined to very small applications and demos (such as the code listings found in books like this). It isn't the recommended approach to take for serious development.

What Is a Module?

A *module* is a collection of controllers, directives, filters, services, and other configuration information. The main player in all this is angular.module, as it is the gateway into the Module API, the mechanism used to configure angular modules. It is used to register, create, and retrieve previously created AngularJS modules.

This probably all sounds rather abstract, so let's look at a practical example by walking through the process of setting up a default module for our application. The default module is the module that AngularJS will use as the entry point into your application. (It may even be the only module you use.) Don't worry if all this doesn't make a lot of sense at the moment, as we will look at a complete listing and talk more about what is happening when we build our custom filter.

Add the following code to a new JavaScript file, which you can name myAppModule.js.

```
// Create a new module
var myAppModule = angular.module('myAppModule', []);
```

You just created a module. Wasn't that easy? The module method was used to create a module named myAppModule. We also captured the returned object (a reference to the module just created) in a variable, also named myAppModule.

You will notice that we also passed an empty array to the module method. This can be used to pass a list of dependencies; that is, other modules that this module depends upon. We don't have any dependencies, so we simply pass an empty array instead.

We now have a module and a reference to this module, so now we can configure it with a custom filter, by adding the following code below the previous line of code:

```
// configure the module with a filter
myAppModule.filter('stripDashes', function() {
        return function(txt) {
          // filter code would go here
        };
});
```

Don't worry too much about the code within the filter method for now. This is something we will see more of when we build a custom filter in the next section. The important part is that you attached a filter to the module. The filter method lets you name your filter (we called this one stripDashes, because, as you will see in the next section, it strips any dashes that might be contained within strings) via its first argument, and it lets you pass in a function as the second argument. We will explore the purpose of this function shortly.

In a similar way, we can also add a controller to our module. In the preceding code, we used the filter method to configure a filter. In the following code, we use the controller method to configure a controller.

```
// configure the module with a controller
myAppModule.controller('MyFilterDemoCtrl', function ($scope) {
        // controller code would go here
    }
);
```

Again, we get to provide a name ('MyFilterDemoCtrl') and pass in a function. This function is basically the same function that we have been using as our controller within the script tags so far, only now it is attached to a module.

If controllers and other logic, such as filters, are created within an AngularJS module, how are they accessed and used? This relates to the AngularJS bootstrapping process. Let's examine that now.

Bootstrapping AngularJS

We talked briefly about the ngApp directive earlier in the book, though we didn't really talk about the role it plays in bootstrapping AngularJS. It might already have occurred to you that AngularJS is hard at work behind the scenes, monitoring form fields, for example, so that it can respond to any changes and immediately update any bindings.

In fact, AngularJS is doing quite a lot behind the scenes, and it all starts to happen once the document is loaded, because it found an ngApp directive. So far, we have used ngApp in its simplest form, as an attribute without any value. However, you can specify an AngularJS default module, by providing a value. The following code snippet shows ngApp with a value of 'myAppModule', which is the name of the module we have just created.

```
<html ng-app="myAppModule">
```

With the ngApp directive in place, we can save our module, myAppModule.js, into the js directory. Then we can create a new page, index.html, which will make use of this module. The next two code listings (Listings 4-8 and Listing 4-9) will pull all of this together.

Listing 4-8. myAppModule.js

```
// create a new module called 'myAppModule' and save
// a reference to it in a variable called myAppModule
var myAppModule = angular.module('myAppModule', []);

// use the myAppModule variable to
// configure the module with a controller
myAppModule.controller('MyFilterDemoCtrl', function ($scope) {
        // controller code would go here
    }
);

// use the myAppModule variable to
// configure the module with a filter
myAppModule.filter('stripDashes', function() {
    return function(txt) {
        // filter code would go here
    };
});
```

Listing 4-8 is the module file in which we create a module and then configure a controller and a filter. Notice that we named the JavaScript file 'myAppModule.js'; we named the variable, which stores a reference to the module 'myAppModule'; and we named the module itself 'myAppModule'. This is not an issue, and it does not always have to be the case that naming follows this pattern. The key thing is to recognize that when we talk about the module, we are talking about the object we created and named when we called the angular.module method. It is this name that we can use to get a reference to the module whenever we need it. To clarify this, Listing 4-9 shows a slightly different approach to setting up and configuring the module.

Listing 4-9. Referring to the Module by Name

```
// Create a new module
angular.module('myAppModule', []);

// configure the module with a controller
angular.module('myAppModule').controller('MyFilterDemoCtrl', function ($scope) {
        // controller code would go here
    }
);

// configure the module with a filter
angular.module('myAppModule'). filter('stripDashes', function() {
    return function(txt) {
        // filter code would go here
    };
});
```

This file does not use a variable to store a reference to the module. Instead, it uses the single argument version of the angular.module method to retrieve a reference to it. This single argument is the name we gave the module when we created it. It really doesn't make much difference which approach you use, and both are commonly used. I prefer the approach in Listing 4-8, where we store a reference, as there is less repetition of the module name, so fewer chances of typos creeping in. Sometimes, however, you might find you need to get a reference to a module, and the single argument version of the module method might be the only way to get it. Now let's turn our attention to Listing 4-10 and the next step in the process.

Listing 4-10. An index.html File Set Up to Use myAppModule

```
<!DOCTYPE html >
<html ng-app="myAppModule">
<head lang="en">
    <meta charset="UTF-8">
    <title>Listing 4-10</title>
    <script src="js/angular.min.js"></script>
    <script src="js/myAppModule.js"></script>
</head>
<body ng-controller="MyFilterDemoCtrl">

</body>
</html>
```

With the default module created, all we have to do now is to associate it with our index.html page. We use ngApp with the name of the module as its value to bootstrap the whole AngularJS process. Take note that we still have to provide a script reference to the myAppModule.js file, so that AngularJS can actually find the module we declared in the ngApp directive.

There is slightly more work in setting up a default module as opposed to lumping everything together in the HTML file, but it's easy enough and soon becomes second nature. You should feel somewhat inspired by the clean look of the index.html page above. As you will see, having the JavaScript file separated from the HTML is well worth the trouble. However, that is not all that we have achieved. We have also set up our application to use the AngularJS module system, and this enables you to tap into all the benefits that go with it.

Creating a Custom Filter

At last, it's time to look at creating a custom filter. Modules are great, but, while important, they're probably not the most exciting topic! This is perhaps because they don't directly produce any visual output. However, custom filters are more exciting, and we are going to use one to solve another issue that we have with our sample data.

For some unknown reason, some values sent back to us are dash delimited. The back end team has told us that this is the way that the data is stored in the database and that it cannot change it. Nonetheless, we aren't very keen on presenting it to our end users in this format. The plan property is an example of this; it has a value of "super-basic-plan". We could easily deal with one case of this without a filter, but we will assume it is a common problem, and we will use a filter to solve it across the whole application.

I find that the best way to go about writing a filter is first to forget about filters. I get the logic working as regular JavaScript, and then I tie it into a filter once I am satisfied. The requirement here is relatively simple: we want to remove any dashes and replace them with spaces. Listing 4-11 shows a basic script that does just what we need.

Listing 4-11. A Simple Replace Dashes Function

```
<script>

    function stripDashes(txt) {
        return txt.split('-').join(' ');
    };

    console.log(stripDashes("super-basic-plan"));
    console.log(stripDashes("something-with-a-lot-more-dashes-plan"));
    console.log(stripDashes("noDashesPlan"));

</script>
```

This function is relatively straightforward. It accepts a single argument—the dash delimited string—and returns the modified string. We have used a few calls to console.log for the purpose of verifying our expectation that it will strip out all of the dashes and leave spaces in their place. The following output suggests this function is fit for this purpose:

```
super basic plan
something with a lot more dashes plan
noDashesPlan
```

> ■ **Tip**   These days, it is increasingly common for JavaScript programmers to write formal unit tests, but we won't explore that topic very much in this book. Realistically, a few calls to the console.log method do not constitute proper testing. As you have chosen to read a book about a framework that fully supports unit testing, I strongly recommend that you read up on the topic in the near future.

As the function is working as we expect it to, we are now ready to convert it to an AngularJS filter. The method we use to create an AngularJS filter is named, unsurprisingly, filter. It accepts two arguments: a name for the filter and a *factory* function. We will name our filter 'stripDashes', and we will create a factory function that returns our stripDashes function. That may have sounded a tad confusing, particularly the bit about factory functions. As usual, a code listing should help clarify. Listing 4-12 is the filter method from Listing 4-9, revised to include the actual filter logic.

Listing 4-12. An Angular Filter Implementation

```
myAppModule.filter('stripDashes', function () {
    // the function we are in returns
    // the function below
    return function(txt) {
        return textToFilter.split('-').join(' ');
    };

});
```

Of particular note here is the fact that the `filter` function does not itself implement our logic; rather, it returns a function that implements it. This is why that second argument supplied to the filter method is called a "factory function"; its main purpose in life is to manufacture functions. This can seem a little strange at first, but it is a common design pattern (generally known as the *factory pattern*), and it's certainly not difficult to implement. It might help if you think about this from AngularJS's point of view: we don't want to use a function here and now, but we do want to *return a function* to AngularJS, for it to utilize whenever we invoke the associated filter.

The argument we named `txt` represents the expression value that is passed in to this filter function when it is used, that is, it's the value we are filtering. In Listing 4-13, which uses our new custom filter, you can see that `txt` will be the value of `data.plan`.

Listing 4-13. Trying Out the `stripDashes` Filter

```
<!DOCTYPE html>
<html>
<head>
    <title>Filter Demo</title>
    <script src="js/angular.min.js"></script>
    <script src="js/myModules/myAppModule.js"></script>
</head>
<body ng-app="myAppModule" ng-controller="MyFilterDemoCtrl">
    <p>Plan type: {{data.plan}}</p>
    <p>Plan type: {{data.plan | stripDashes}}</p>
</body>
</html>
```

There you have it, a very handy filter that we can reuse across our application. As an additional example, let's create another filter. As I mentioned earlier in the chapter, we can improve upon the way we handle the `firstName` and `surname` by using a technique known as *title casing*, instead of simply converting them to lowercase. We can do this by making sure the first character is in uppercase and all of the remaining characters are in lowercase. As before, let's first write the code that will accomplish this, before we create the filter itself. Have a look at Listing 4-14.

Listing 4-14. A Basic Title Casing Function

```
<script>

    function toTitleCase(str)
    {
        return str.charAt(0).toUpperCase() + str.substr(1).toLowerCase();
    }
```

```
    console.log(toTitleCase("jennifer"));
    console.log(toTitleCase("jENniFEr"));
    console.log(toTitleCase("jENniFEr amanda Grant"));
</script>
```

Let's have a look at the output of Listing 4-14 and see if it meets our needs.

```
Jennifer
Jennifer
Jenni.amanda grant
```

It's a fairly simple function, and it does what we need it to do. That is to say, it will indeed convert the firstName and surname to title case. It does so by using the string method's charAt() method to access and convert the first character to uppercase (as returned by str.charAt(0).toUpperCase()) and concatenating the resulting value to a lowercased portion of the string that consists of all but the first character (as returned by str.substr(1).toLowerCase()).

However, I don't like the fact that this function works only on the very first word when it is given a multiple word string as an argument. While we could perhaps get away with this for the cases in which we only want to work with a single word, it is not a very forward-thinking approach. Let's add the ability to handle multiple words (see Listing 4-15).

Listing 4-15. A Better Title Casing Function

```
<script>

    function toTitleCase(str)
    {
        return str.replace(/\w\S*/g, function(txt){return txt.charAt(0).toUpperCase() + txt.
        substr(1).toLowerCase();});
    }

    console.log(toTitleCase("jennifer"));
    console.log(toTitleCase("jENniFEr"));
    console.log(toTitleCase("jENniFEr amanda Grant"));

</script>
```

The following output shows that this is a better implementation. The last line now shows that each word has had its first character converted to uppercase.

```
Jennifer
Jennifer
Jennifer Amanda Grant
```

Of course, the function is now a little more complicated. The trick to understanding it lies in the use of the string object's replace() method. This method is very powerful, but it does require some knowledge of regular expressions before you can truly master it. A regular expression is a sequence of symbols and characters expressing a pattern to be searched for within a longer piece of text. The first argument to this method is a regular expression, which looks like this: /\w\S*/g. More specifically, in this particular case, it is looking for each individual word. The anonymous function, which is the second argument, is executed for each word that is found. This function uses the same logic you saw in Listing 4-12; therefore, each word now has its first character converted to uppercase and all remaining characters converted to lower case.

Now we will use this approach to create another filter in the module we created in Listing 4-9. We will name this one toTitleCase. This is shown in Listing 4-16.

Listing 4-16. An Angular Filter Implementation

```
myAppModule.filter("toTitleCase", function () {
    return function (str) {
        return str.replace(/\w\S*/g, function(txt){ return txt.charAt(0).toUpperCase() + txt.
        substr(1).toLowerCase();});
    };
});
```

With the filter in place, we can now make use of it. Listing 4-17 shows it in action. In this example, we show the filter working on individual words (firstName and surname), and we also see it in action on a concatenation of firstName and surname.

Listing 4-17. Using the toTitleCase Filter

```
<!DOCTYPE html>
<html>
<head>
    <title>Filter Demo</title>
    <script src="js/angular.min.js"></script>
    <script src="js/myModules/myAppModule.js"></script>
</head>
<body ng-app="myAppModule" ng-controller="MyFilterDemoCtrl">
<!-- Display customer name in title case -->
<p>First Name: {{data.firstName | toTitleCase}}</p>
<p>Surname: {{data.surname | toTitleCase}}</p>
<p>Full Name: {{ data.firstName + data.surname | toTitleCase}}</p>
</body></html>
```

Summary

We looked at both filters and modules in this chapter, and you learned how they relate to each other. AngularJS ships with some handy built-in filters, and you now know how to create your own. You can also benefit from filters that have been made available online (such as those found at http://ngmodules.org/).

Modules gave us something to "attach" our filter to, and you also learned that modules are AngularJS's preferred mechanism for packaging and organizing code. We will take the module approach for the rest of the book, so there is still plenty of time to see them in action, should the topic still seem a little hazy.

CHAPTER 5

Directives

Most JavaScript frameworks have a "special something" that sets them apart. That special something in the case of AngularJS is undoubtedly directives. The idea that we can use a declarative approach that lets us augment HTML with new capabilities has great appeal. I suspect this has very much to do with clean looks and intuitive syntax, but it might be because it is a fun and enjoyable way to approach client-side web development.

In this chapter, I will recap some of the things we have already been using, by looking at the built-in directives. You will also have a first look at creating custom directives.

Directives, in Angular JS, are essentially JavaScript functions that are invoked when the Document Object Model (DOM) is compiled by the Angular JS framework. I will touch on what is meant by the DOM being "compiled" when we take a peek behind the scenes later in the chapter, but for now, it is enough to know that directives are "attached" to their corresponding DOM elements when the document is loaded.

■ **Tip** Don't let the word *compiler* scare you off! It is simply AngularJS terminology for the internal mechanism that is used to associate directives with HTML elements.

Due to this this powerful concept, Angular JS lets you create totally new directives that we can use to encapsulate logic and simplify DOM manipulation—directives that can modify or even create totally new behavior in HTML.

What can we use directives for? As directives can modify or even create totally new behavior, we can use directives for anything from simple reusable blocks of static content right through to sophisticated client-side user interfaces with network and database connectivity—and everything else in between. The built-in directives provide the general level of functionality that you would expect to find—the bread-and-butter directives, so to speak—though custom directives let you push things much further. The only limit is your imagination. (Well, maybe your JavaScript skills have some impact on this too!)

Of course, Angular JS is much more than directives; however, they do seem to be the main attraction. I hope, by the end of this chapter, you will have gained an appreciation of why this is so.

The Basics of Directives

What do directives look like? You are no doubt thinking that you have seen enough in use so far to know the answer to that question. It may surprise you to learn that directives can take on a few different forms. Let's pick on the ngController directive as an example.

As you know, the ngController directive looks like the following:

```
<div ng-controller="myFilterDemoCtrl"></div>
```

This is a typical directive declaration, and it is by far the most common way to use directives: that is, as an attribute. One potential issue with this approach is that the document that contains it will not validate as HTML5-compliant. If this is a concern to you, or your organization, you can do the following instead:

```
<div data:ng-controller="myFilterDemoCtrl"></div>
```

This is very similar to the approach to which we are accustomed, though here we use the prefix data: before our directive name. Validators are happy with this, because it uses a standard approach to creating custom data attributes.

In both the preceding cases, we invoke the directive using an attribute, though this is not our only option. All of the following methods are also technically possible:

As an attribute:

```
<span my-directive></span>
```

As an element:

```
<my-directive></my-directive>
```

As a class:

```
<span class="my-directive: expression;"></span>
```

As a comment:

```
<!-- directive: my-directive expression -->
```

I say "technically possible," because directives authors may or may not have enabled their directives to be used in all possible forms. You will learn more about this when we build a custom directive later in this chapter. In reality, you won't use the last two options, as they exist mainly for use with much older browsers, and you will rarely see them in use in the wild. Still, it's nice to have options, and at least you won't be caught unawares if you should stumble upon any of these.

Using Directives

A directive is rarely an island unto itself. That is to say, directives often need to communicate and interact with the rest of your application. This is usually done through a scope, as you have seen in previous chapters. Let's start building a small part of an application that shows this idea in action.

Listing 5-1 shows `product-detail.html`. This is the HTML and CSS code for a product selection page. We will focus our efforts on an exciting new fictitious product: the AngularJS socks. These amazing socks, created specifically to warm the feet of AngularJS developers, come in a variety of colors. The requirement here is to hide the list of available colors until the customer is ready to choose one. The directives we will use to achieve all of this are `ngClick`, `ngHide`, and `ngController`.

■ **Note**   It is an established convention in the Angular world to refer to directives using CamelCase when writing about them. For example, we would write `ngController`, as I do in the preceding paragraph. This can be a little confusing, because to use a directive in code, you must use the dash-delimited form of its name. For example, we would code the aforementioned directive as `ng-controller`. You will see this convention in practice when you view the official Angular documentation or read other books on the topic.

The bulk of this code is the CSS, which, for the most part, sets up the colors for the associated `div` elements. You will see that, due to the `ng-hide="isHidden"` directive placed on each of these `div` elements, the page defaults to a state in which the color list is hidden.

Listing 5-1. `product-detail.html`, a Basic Product Detail Page

```html
<!DOCTYPE html >
<html ng-app="myAppModule">
<head>
    <title></title>
    <script src="js/angular.js"></script>
    <script src="js/myAppModule.js"></script>
    <style>

        body {
            font-family: "Lucida Grande", "Lucida Sans Unicode", Helvetica, Arial, sans-serif;
        }

        div {
            margin: 20px;
            padding: 20px;
            font-size: 16px;
            color:#ffffff;
        }

        #red {
            background-color: red;
        }

        #green {
            background-color: green;
        }

        #blue {
            background-color: blue;
        }
```

```
        #purple {
            background-color: purple;
        }

        #gray {
            background-color: gray;
        }

        #olive {
            background-color: olive;
        }


    </style>
</head>
<body ng-controller="myProductDetailCtrl">

<h2>AngularJS Socks</h2>

<p>Keep warm this winter with our 100% wool, 100% cool, AngularJS socks!</p>

<button ng-click="showHideColors()" type="button">
    {{isHidden ? 'Show Available Colors' : 'Hide Available Colors'}}
</button>

<div id="red" ng-hide="isHidden">Red</div>
<div id="green" ng-hide="isHidden">Green</div>
<div id="blue" ng-hide="isHidden">Blue</div>
<div id="purple" ng-hide="isHidden">Purple</div>
<div id="gray" ng-hide="isHidden">Dark Slate Gray</div>
<div id="olive" ng-hide="isHidden">Olive</div>

</body>
</html>
```

Figure 5-1 shows how this page looks when it first loads. A product description and a button that will show or hide the available colors when clicked are displayed.

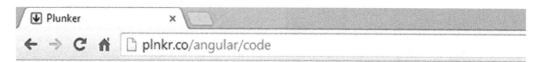

Figure 5-1. *The default view of product-detail.html>*

As available space on today's screens can be quite limited, it is incredibly useful to be able to hide information and to make it available on demand. Figure 5-2 shows how it looks when the Show Available Colors button is clicked.

Figure 5-2. *The Show Available Colors view of* product-detail.html

The interesting thing about this implementation is how the logic is assembled. It's intuitive, and it doesn't leave a trail of messy JavaScript code in its wake. In fact, the product-detail.html file is primarily HTML and CSS code. Ofcourse, there must be some JavaScript code somewhere. I'm hoping that, with last chapter's coverage of modules in mind (and the ng-app="myAppModule" directive on the second line), you already know where this JavaScript is. It is tucked away in a module file. Let's have a look at this module now (see Listing 5-2).

Listing 5-2. The myAppModule.js Application Module

```
// Create the module
angular.module('myAppModule', []);

// configure the module with a controller
angular.module('myAppModule').controller('myProductDetailCtrl', function ($scope) {

        // Hide colors by default
        $scope.isHidden = true;
```

```
    // a function, placed into the scope, which
    // can toggle the value of the isHidden variable
    $scope.showHideColors = function () {
        $scope.isHidden = !$scope.isHidden;
    }

  }
);
```

It's surprisingly short, mainly because we don't actually do very much heavy lifting ourselves. Instead, we concentrate on managing the state of the isHidden variable. The ngHide directive is taking care of how the underlying task is actually implemented.

As you may have come to expect by now, we are utilizing the scope object. Consequently, the isHidden variable and the showHideColors() function can be used in the directives expressions. These two actions constitute the wiring up of our logic.

Take a look at the following excerpts from the product-detail.html file from Listing 5-1. You can see where the showHideColors() function that we assigned to the scope is used by ngClick

```
<button ng-click="showHideColors()" type="button">
    {{isHidden ? 'Show Available Colors' : 'Hide Available Colors'}}
</button>
```

. . . and where the isHidden variable we assigned to the scope is used by ngHide

```
<div id="red" ng-hide="isHidden">Red</div>
```

■ **Tip**   Just a reminder: There is no need to specify the $scope object within these Angular expressions, as expressions are implicitly associated with a scope. Attempting to do, say, "$scope.isHidden" in the above expression would not work.

Why are all of the color divs hidden by default? This is because the expression, isHidden, provided to the ngHide directive on each of the divs evaluates to true. What is really cool, due to the live updating that Angular JS performs, is that anytime the value of isHidden changes, ngHide will respond accordingly. Of course, we want it to change, and that is why we use the Show Available Colors button along with the ngClick directive.

The button uses the ngClick directive, and the expression we pass to this directive is a call to our showHideColors() function. It is this function call that will change the state of the isHidden variable, thereby causing the ngHide directive's expression now to evaluate to false. Consequently, the color divs become visible.

An interesting requirement in the case of the button is that we want the text to adapt when the button is clicked. We do this using a particularly helpful technique that can be used within Angular JS expressions. I'm referring to the following line:

```
{{isHidden ? 'Show Available Colors' : 'Hide Available Colors'}}
```

This expression uses the ternary conditional operator. It can look a little odd if you haven't seen it before, but it's actually quite easy to use. The first portion, the bit before the ? (question mark), must evaluate to true or false. If it evaluates to true, the statement before the : (colon) is executed; otherwise, the one after it is executed. In our case, the text appearing on the button will update itself, based on whether or not the color divs are currently hidden, because we use isHidden to drive the outcome.

For a relatively small amount of code, we get a fairly useful piece of functionality. This shows how directives can be greater than the sum of their parts. It also shows, I hope, that directives can lead to well-encapsulated code that can keep complexity out of sight. We can do even better still, but we will get to that when I cover custom directives in the last section of this chapter.

Built-in Directives

In this section, we will take a look at a few very useful built-in directives. We can't look at all of them here, as it would take far too long. However, I would like to give you a sense of the directives that ship with the framework and some examples of how they work. I won't pay much attention to HTML form-related directives, as these get their own coverage in the next chapter.

ngBind

Much of the time, you don't use ngBind directly, because the double curly braces achieve the same thing. For example, the following two code snippets are functionally equivalent:

```
<span ng-bind="2+2"></span>
```

```
{{2+2}}
```

Both ngBind and the expression syntax ask Angular JS to display the value of a given expression and update the output accordingly when the value of that expression changes.

If we have expressions, why bother to use ngBind? A benefit of using the ngBind approach relates to the fact that, if a document takes some time to load, your HTML page might temporarily show the raw expressions to your end users. That is to say, they may literally see the {{2+2}} appear momentarily before Angular JS gets a chance to compile it and show the desired values. Using ngBind does not have this unfortunate side effect.

You probably don't want to give up using the curly brace syntax, so keep reading. The ngCloak directive is here to save the day.

ngCloak

If your document is taking time to load, and you are noticing issues with the raw expressions that are appearing, you don't have to use the ngBind approach mentioned previously. You can use ngCloak instead. This directive is shown in action following:

```
<p ng-cloak>{{ 2 + 2 }}</p>
```

Here we "cloak" the Angular expression simply by declaring ngCloak (no value is required for this attribute). The cloaking of the expression happens because ngCloak applies a CSS rule that hides it, although it is only hidden until Angular JS has determined that it can display the evaluated value.

It is tempting simply to add this directive to the body element, so that it applies to the whole document hierarchy, but often this is not a good idea. This would prevent the browser's natural desire to render the page progressively. Instead, it is often better to apply it on individual elements. Better yet, if your document is not large enough to be exhibiting this undesirable behavior, don't use it at all!

ngInclude

This handy directive lets you include the contents of another file within your document. Take, for example, the very small file in Listing 5-3, which we have named include-me.html.

Listing 5-3. include-me.html

```
<p>Thanks for visiting our website!</p>
```

Now, let's include this file's output at the bottom of includes-in-action.html (see Listing 5-4).

Listing 5-4. includes-in-action.html

```
<!DOCTYPE html>
<html>
<head>
    <title></title>
</head>
<body>
<h1>Includes in Action</h1>

    <p> You should see the inluded files contents below</p>
    <div ng-include="'include-me.html'"></div>

</body>
</html>
```

This directive is easy to use, but there is one potential pain point for the Angular JS beginner. Be aware that ngInclude expects to be supplied with an Angular JS expression. Remember, an Angular JS expression is a subset of JavaScript, and it follows all the usual rules. A string must either be single-quoted or double-quoted. As the Angular JS expression is itself double-quoted, the string you provide within it must be single-quoted. This is why we use "'include-me.html'". Using "include-me.html" simply wouldn't work.

▪ **Note**   The ngInclude directive has additional options, which we will examine further when I talk about animations, in Chapter 9.

---

ngShow and ngHide

The ngShow directive will show or hide the HTML element upon which it is defined. The element is shown or hidden by adding or removing a predefined AngularJS class called ng-hide. The p element in the following example will be shown only when $scope.correctAnswer is true.

```
<p ng-show="correctAnswer">That answer is correct!</p>
```

If we assume that $scope.correctAnswer is false; looking at the source code of the HTML page would reveal that the ngHide class has been added to the p element by the AngularJS framework.

```
<p ng-show="isCorrectAnswer" class="ng-hide">That answer is correct!</p>
```

The ng-hide class is very simple and nothing more than a single CSS rule, as follows.

```
.ng-hide{
  display: none !important;
}
```

As you might imagine, the ngHide directive does the exact opposite. The following example achieves the same result as the previous example, but by asking the question in a different way. Here, the text within the p element is hidden when $scope.correctAnswer is *not* true.

```
<p ng-hide="!correctAnswer">That answer is correct!</p>
```

ngRepeat

The ngRepeat directive is definitely one of the most useful built-in directives. It is, essentially, a looping construct that instantiates a template once for every item in a collection (for example, an array). It also has a number of useful built-in variables, which are shown in Table 5-1.

Table 5-1. ngRepeat Built-in Variables

Variable Name	Type	Description
$index	Number	Iterator offset of the repeated element (0..length-1)
$first	Boolean	True, if the repeated element is first in the iterator
$middle	Boolean	True, if the repeated element is between first and last in the iterator
$last	Boolean	True, if the repeated element is last in the iterator
$even	Boolean	True, if the iterator position $index is even (otherwise, false)
$odd	Boolean	True, if the iterator position $index is odd (otherwise, false)

Let's have a look at a code listing (Listing 5-5) that puts ngRepeat and some of these built-in variables to use.

Listing 5-5. Using ngRepeat with Some of the Built-in Variables

```
<h2>My Favourite Cities</h2>
<div ng-repeat="city in ['Liverpool','Perth','Sydney','Dublin','Paris']">

    {{$index}}. {{city}}
    {{$first ? '(This is the first row)' : ''}} {{$last ? '(This is the last row)' : ''}}

</div>
```

The output can be seen in Figure 5-3. The $index variable gives us the row numbers, and we use $first and $last to output conditionally, whether or not we are on the first or last row, respectively. The most important thing to understand about this ngRepeat example is the format of the expression with which we provide it.

```
"city in ['Liverpool','Perth','Sydney','Dublin','Paris']"
```

This format follows the *variable in collection* pattern. I chose the name "city" for the variable, and the collection is the array of cities. Another important thing to know about ngRepeat is that it creates, at each pass through the loop, a new scope object, each one quite distinct from the controller's own $scope object. In fact, this is why we can have different values for variables, such as $index and city.

My Favourite Cities

0. Liverpool (This is the first row)
1. Perth
2. Sydney
3. Dublin
4. Paris (This is the last row)

Figure 5-3. *Repeating with ngRepeat*

Event-Handling Directives

We have seen ngClick already, though Angular JS comes with similar directives for handling the usual browser events, such as ondblclick, onblur, onfocus, and onsubmit. Each directive works pretty much as you would expect and is named using the same format. So, for the list of events I just mentioned, we would have the corresponding Angular JS versions: ngDblclick, ngBlur, ngFocus, and ngSubmit.

You don't have to use these directives, as Angular JS in no way prevents you from using the regular JavaScript event handlers. However, it is generally recommended that you do use them, especially if you want to stay within the Angular JS framework. For example, a big difference between regular events and their Angular JS equivalents is that the equivalents take Angular JS expressions. This means that you have access to the implicitly available $scope object, among other things.

Using the API Documentation

There are far more directives than I can cover here, though all of them are well-documented at https://docs. angularjs.org/api/ng/directive/. This documentation is quite good, though it can be a little terse at times. It is well worth familiarizing yourself with it. Following is a brief guide to how it is usually presented (see Table 5-2).

Table 5-2. *Information Available Through the Online API Documentation*

Directive Name and Overview	The directive's name, for example; ngRepeat
Directive Info	Additional information, such as the priority level, which may impact the behavior of the directive
Usage	This corresponds to our discussion of how a directive can be used. For example, some directives can be used only as an attribute.
Arguments	This tells you if the argument(s) should be an Angular JS expression, a string, or some other value.
Example	A brief example of the directive in action

I wish I could say that all of the answers are to be found in the API documentation, but many of the problems that I see posted in online forums are indeed readily available here. If you run into problems, or you just want to look up some more directives, it should certainly be at the top of your list of places to go to find help.

Creating a Custom Directive

While there are plenty of built-in directives, you will occasionally need to build your own application-specific directives. In this section, we will look at an example that should serve to get you up to speed on the basics of how to do just that. Custom directives can seem a bit intimidating at first, mainly because there are a lot of moving parts.

My aim here is to get you up to speed with the basics and put you in good shape to tackle the more advanced aspects as and when you need them. To achieve this, we will create a custom directive that we will call colorList. This directive will encapsulate much of the code we looked at in Listing 5-1. To recap, this produced a color selection list, which could be activated and deactivated using a button. Listing 5-6 shows how this directive can be used within the product-detail.html file.

Listing 5-6. The colorList Directive in Use

```
<!DOCTYPE html >
<html ng-app="myAppModule">
 <head>
   <title>A Custom Directive</title>
   <script src="js/angular.min.js"></script>
   <script src="myAppModule.js"></script>
 </head>
 <body ng-controller="myDemoCtrl">
   <h2>AngularJS Socks</h2>
   <p>Keep warm this winter with our 100% wool, 100% cool, AngularJS socks!</p>

   <div color-list colors="colorsArray"></div>

</body>
</html>
```

As you can see, it's quite easy to use this directive. It looks and behaves in the same way as product-detail. html. It houses a button that is used to show and hide the available colors, but rather than hard-code the colors using manually crafted div elements, as we did earlier, we will make this directive much more reusable, by using a colors attribute. This allows us to pass in an array of colors, so that we can determine which colors to use on a case-by-case basis.

Like filters and controllers, directives are configured on a module. Let's examine how this works (see Listing 5-7). It should look relatively familiar.

Listing 5-7. Configuring a Directive

```
myAppModule.directive('colorList', function () {

    return {

        restrict: 'AE',
        template:
            "<button ng-click='showHideColors()' type='button'>"
          + "{{isHidden ? 'Show Available Colors' : 'Hide Available Colors'}}"
          + "</button><div ng-hide='isHidden' id='colorContainer'>"
          + "</div>"

    }
});
```

We'll build on this until our directive is fully implemented, but for now, let's focus on what is achieved in Listing 5-7. Using the directive method on the module, we have registered a directive with the Angular JS framework. We named this directive, via the first argument, colorList. The second argument is an anonymous function, which returns a *directive definition object*. This is a regular JavaScript object that we need to set up with various properties that tell Angular JS all about our directive. So far, all that we have configured is the restrict and template options. Let's deal with restrict first.

The restrict Option

The restrict option is used to specify how a directive can be invoked. As you saw earlier, there are four different ways to invoke a directive. This corresponds to the four valid options for restrict.

Table 5-3 provides an example of each valid option. As our directive uses the value 'AE'; this means that it can be invoked as either an attribute or an element. As I mentioned earlier in this chapter, you won't use the last two options, C and M, as they exist mainly for use with much older browsers.

Table 5-3. *Valid restrict Options*

Option	Example
A	`<span color-list ></span>`
E	`<color-list></color-list>`
C	`<span class="color-list"></span>`
M	`<!-- directive: color-list -->`

When should you use an element and when should you use an attribute? You can use either, and the end result will be the same. However, the Angular team recommends that you use an element when you are creating a component that is in control of the template and an attribute when you are decorating an existing element with new functionality.

The template Option

As the name suggests, the `template` option lets you define a template. The template is appended to your directive declaration by default (though there is a `replace` option that allows you to replace the element on which the directive occurs entirely). Let's consider the HTML code that I have provided as the value to the `template` option. I have shown this again in Listing 5-8, but, this time, without the string quotations, so it is easier to read.

Listing 5-8. The Value of the `template` Option

```
<button ng-click='showHideColors()' type='button'>
 {{isHidden ? 'Show Available Colors' : 'Hide Available Colors'}}
</button>
<div ng-hide='isHidden' id='colorContainer'></div>
```

You will recognize the button and the expression within it. The `div` with the id of `colorContainer` is new. This is because we will abandon the approach of hard-coding the color `div`s manually in favor of dynamically appending them to this `div`, based on array values. We will see this in action shortly.

■ **Tip** I've kept things together here for convenience, but there is an additional option for templates in the `templateUrl` option. This lets you move the source code for your template into a separate file. This is then loaded via Ajax. For longer templates, this is usually better than using the `template` option, as all you have to provide is the URL to this file.

Of particular note here is that the template contains Angular JS code, such as the `ng-click` directive and the expression that renders the button text. Thus, your templates can be as simple or as complex as you need them to be.

With `restrict` and `template` covered, we now require a way to tell Angular JS about our underlying logic. This logic appeared in our controller function earlier, but now we need to encapsulate it within this custom directive. One way to do this is to use the `link` option.

The link Option

The function that you assign to the `link` option is where the main action takes place. This function has access to the current scope (by default) and the element on which the directive was declared (the `div` element, in this case). For clarity, let's list precisely what we want this directive to achieve. This will make it easier to follow the rationale behind the implemented logic. The directive should perform the following:

1. Add a button to the page. This button will be a toggle for showing and hiding a list of colors.

2. By default, the color list should be hidden.

3. The colors should be shown as `div` elements that can display a color and color name, based on an array of strings corresponding to that color.

4. The color list should be an array containing CSS color name values. This should be available within the directive.

We need a `link` function that achieves all but one of these requirements. The first requirement is already met, because the button is defined in the HTML we assigned through the `template` option. The second requirement is partially met, but it still needs work. I say *partially* met, because the template also has the `colorContainer div`, which will be the parent container for our color list. This `div` makes use of the `ngHide` directive.

Listing 5-9 shows our `link` function. This function completes the requirements we listed earlier. I will put this in context with the rest of our custom directive shortly, but for now, see if you can pick out what is happening here.

Listing 5-9. The `link` Function

```
link: function ($scope, $element) {

    // set default state of hide/show
    $scope.isHidden = true;
    // add function to manage hide/show state
    $scope.showHideColors = function () {
        $scope.isHidden = !$scope.isHidden;
    }

    // DOM manipulation
    var colorContainer = $element.find('div');
    angular.forEach($scope.$parent.colorsArray, function (color) {
        var appendString = "<div style='background-color:" + color + "'>" + color + "</div>";
        colorContainer.append(appendString);             });

}
```

The first thing to notice about the `link` function is that we have access to the element on which the directive is defined and a scope object (via the `$element` and `$scope` arguments accepted by the function). These are automatically injected into our function by the framework.

The first batch of logic in this function simply sets the default state of the directive such that the color list is hidden. Next, we attach the `showHideColors()` function to the scope. The next batch of logic, under the DOM manipulation comment, is the real meat of the directive.

We want to add `div` elements dynamically to the `colorContainer div`, so we create a variable called `colorContainer`. To achieve this, we used the following statement:

```
var colorContainer = $element.find('div');
```

If you have used jQuery before, this might look familiar. This is because `$element` is a jQuery wrapped element and, as such, can use jQuery methods, such as `find()` and `append()`.

■ **Note** By default, Angular JS uses jqLite. This is a trimmed-down version of jQuery containing only the most essential features. If you add a script reference to the full version of jQuery, Angular will automatically use this version instead of using jqLite. If you are keen to learn what jqLite has to offer, you can do so here: `https://docs.angularjs.org/api/ng/function/angular.element`.

With the `colorContainer` reference in hand, we can now create the color list by attaching to it a `div` for each color in the array. We do this by looping through the colors array, using the handy `angular.forEach` method and, at each pass, append to build the list of colors.

Within the forEach loop, we do the append operation by creating a div element as a string value that is constructed using the current array item (the CSS color name). This is used as both the value of the background-color CSS rule and as the literal text that displays within the div.

```
var appendString = "<div style='background-color:" + color + "'>" + color + "</div>";
colorContainer.append(appendString);
```

Both the HTML page that uses the directive and the module that contains the directive and controller code are shown in Listing 5-10 and Listing 5-11, respectively.

Listing 5-10. product-detail.html, Revised to Use a Custom Directive

```
<!DOCTYPE html >
<html ng-app="myAppModule">
<head>
    <title></title>
    <script src="https://ajax.googleapis.com/ajax/libs/angularjs/1.2.21/angular.min.js"></script>
    <script src="/compass/src/js/myAppModule.js"></script>
    <style>
        #colorContainer div {
            color: white;
            text-transform: uppercase;
            width: 200px;
            padding: 10px;
            margin:5px;
            border-radius: 5px;
            -moz-border-radius: 5px;
        }
    </style>

</head>
<body ng-controller="myDemoCtrl">
<h2>AngularJS Socks</h2>
<p>Keep warm this winter with our 100% wool, 100% cool, AngularJS socks!</p>
        <div color-list colors="colorsArray"></div>
</body>
</html>
```

Listing 5-11. The Application Module Containing Our Directive Registration and Our Controller

```
// declare a module
var myAppModule = angular.module('myAppModule', []);


myAppModule.controller('myDemoCtrl', function ($scope) {
        $scope.colorsArray = ['red', 'green', 'blue', 'purple', 'olive']
    }
);


myAppModule.directive('colorList', function ($compile) {
```

```
    return {

        restrict: 'AE',
        template: "<button ng-click='showHideColors()' type='button'>"
            + "{{isHidden ? 'Show Available Colors' : 'Hide Available Colors'}}"
            + "</button><div ng-hide='isHidden' id='colorContainer'>"
            + "</div>",
        link: function ($scope, $element) {

            // set default state of hide/show
            $scope.isHidden = true;
            // add function to manage hide/show state
            $scope.showHideColors = function () {
                $scope.isHidden = !$scope.isHidden;
            }

            // add colors divs to the document
            var colorContainer = $element.find('div');
            angular.forEach($scope.colorsArray, function (color) {
                var appendString = "<div style='background-color:" + color + "'>" + color +   "</
div>";

                colorContainer.append(appendString);
            });
        }
    };

});
```

This is not bad for a first directive—though I think you will agree that there are quite a few steps involved! To keep things manageable, I set up the background color using an inline style, but you might want to create a style sheet with a class and use that class here instead. This is certainly much better practice in most cases. Custom directives are a topic worthy of their own book. Nevertheless, even with this brief introduction, you can build all sorts of reusable logic and user-interface components. I encourage you to explore this topic further, perhaps using some of the many online tutorials or the excellent book *Pro AngularJS* by Adam Freeman (Apress, 2014).

Summary

Directives in AngularJS are *very* powerful, but it can take some time to understand all of the processes that lie behind them completely—particularly when it comes to creating custom directives. In this chapter, you had a good first look at many aspects of directives and, I hope, gained a solid footing on which to base further exploration.

In the next chapter, we will look at another area where AngularJS really shines: HTML forms. While HTML forms are not an AngularJS feature as such, you will appreciate how much more enjoyable and productive AngularJS makes them.

CHAPTER 6

Working with Forms

Since their introduction in the mid-90s, HTML forms have taken a largely static World Wide Web and turned it into a place of business and a rich source of interactivity and entertainment. Initially, HTML forms were functionally limited and clunky, but the specification evolved, and developers learned to work around the issues. Today, thanks in large part to frameworks such as AngularJS, HTML forms are the underlying reason that web-based applications now rival traditional desktop applications. To put all of this more concisely: HTML forms cannot be ignored!

In this chapter, we will look at how to use AngularJS with forms and how to perform tasks such as model binding and data validation. Fortunately, AngularJS doesn't require that you learn about forms from scratch, as it simply enhances the way forms already work, although these enhancements are not always obvious or intuitive. Before we get into all that, however, let's start with a brief recap of what standard forms offer us.

HTML Forms Overview

I could probably devote a couple of chapters to forms, but I won't do that, as our focus is, of course, AngularJS. However, what I do provide here is a relatively brief recap of the basics. If you have already mastered forms, feel free to skip ahead.

■ **Note** AngularJS relies upon some relatively new, though well supported, HTML5 features when working with forms. If you are concerned about older browsers, you should pay extra attention to how your forms behave when testing.

The *form* Element

The form element itself is a good place to begin. This element defines the form as a whole, and it is a responsible mechanism for telling the web browser what to do once the user presses the submit button. For instance, where should it send the data that was collected, and what method should it use to send this data? It does this via its action and method attributes, respectively.

```
<form name="myForm" action="myserver/someaction" method="post">
   ...

</form>
```

The form in the preceding code snippet is configured to use the `post` method and to submit its data to `myserver/somescript.php`. Besides the `method` and `action` attributes that set these values, there is a `name` attribute that we have set to `"myForm"`. In AngularJS, it is quite likely that the `name` attribute will be far more important to you than the other form element attributes. Why is this? In short, it is because developers tend to use Ajax to send data to the server, and they often do not rely on the `form` element's attributes to determine how the Ajax operation is carried out. (I discuss this further in the next chapter.) Setting a name on the form will give you access to some very worthwhile AngularJS features, which we will examine shortly.

■ **Tip** Ajax is a group of technologies used in combination. However, JavaScript developers often use the term to refer to the use of JavaScript for exchanging data asynchronously between a browser and server to avoid full-page reloads.

Of course, a form is no good without `form`-related elements nested within it, so let's look at these next. We'll start with the very versatile `input` element.

The *input* Element

The `input` element is the `form` workhorse. You can use it to create text fields, check boxes, radio buttons, and more. It all hinges on what you specify as the value of its `type` attribute. Its possible values include the following:

```
button
checkbox
file
hidden
image
password
radio
reset
submit
text
```

Following, we will look at the most frequently used of these attributes.

button

This is a simple clickable button that doesn't actually do anything if left to its own devices. It is usually used along with JavaScript to implement some sort of custom behavior. Here's how you create one:

```
<input name="save-button" type="button" value="Click me"/>
```

submit

This is a button too. However, unlike `button`, this has built-in functionality associated with it. This `submit` button triggers the browser to gather up and submit all of the form's data and send it along to its destination. The destination is the value of the action attribute that was declared on the `form` element. An important point here is that only the data within the form that the `submit` button resides in is sent along to the destination. This makes perfect sense when you consider that you can have more than one form on your page. Here's what it looks like:

```
<input type="submit" name="submit" value="Register"/>
```

It is the `value` attribute that determines the text that appears on the button. The `name` attribute can be used as a reference. For example, you might use this in JavaScript code or in the server-side processing logic (such as a PHP script), once the form is submitted. This attribute applies to all of the `form` elements and serves the same purpose in each case.

text

By far the most commonly used input type, the `text` input creates a single-line box into which the user can enter text. Here's what it looks like:

```
<input placeholder="First Name" type="text" name="first-name" size="20"/>
```

In this example, I used the `placeholder` attribute to create a hint as to the expected value of this field. Using `placeholder` can be a very efficient way of exploiting available screen space, as it can be used in lieu of a label. The `size` attribute dictates the width of the field. I rarely use this attribute, as I tend to use CSS instead, which gives much more precision and control. Here's an example using this approach:

```
<input placeholder="First Name" type="text" name="first-name" style="width: 220px;"/>
```

Here, I have used the `style` attribute to inline a CSS rule and set the width property to 220 pixels. Inlining the CSS rule like this is good for demonstrations, but, of course, you could (and probably should) use a dedicated style sheet for all of your CSS rules.

■ **Caution**   I mentioned previously that the `placeholder` attribute can be a very efficient way of exploiting available screen space. However, it can create accessibility issues. Using the `label` element is generally a better approach. The `label` element, covered later in this section, is also much better supported across browsers.

---

checkbox

If you want your users to respond with a yes or no, a true or false, or some other two state values, `checkbox` is the input type that you need. The only possible actions are checking or unchecking the box. Here's what the check box looks like:

```
<input type="checkbox" name="chknewsletter" value="opt-in-newsletter"/>
```

The `value` attribute determines the value that is sent to the server. For example, you can set the value to `opt-in-newsletter`, and this is the string value that will be sent to the server as the checked value.

Following is another, almost identical, example. In this case, we have added the checked attribute, so that the check box will be in its checked state by default.

```
<input type="checkbox" name="chknewsletter" value="opt-in-newsletter" checked/>
```

password

The `password` field is very similar to the standard text input. It looks like this:

```
<input type="password" name="pin" id="pin">
```

The `password` input differs in that the characters entered into it are masked in the browser, so that prying eyes cannot read what is being entered.

radio

The radio button control is perhaps the trickiest input type. Named after the old-fashioned radio sets, which used buttons instead of a dial (or a scan function such as we have on modern radios), tuning among stations was accomplished by using a series of buttons that were pre-tuned to certain stations. Pressing down on one button caused any other depressed button to pop back up. It is the same with radio buttons on the Web; that is, you can "depress," or choose, only one button at any given time.

For this system to work, though, each radio button in the group from which you want your users to choose must have the same name. In Listing 6-1, you can see that each radio button has been given a name of "station".

Listing 6-1. A Group of radio Buttons

```
<div>
  <input type="radio" name="station" id="rad1" value="triple-m"/> <label for="rad1">Triple M</label>
</div>

<div>
  <input type="radio" name="station" id="rad2" value="today-fm"/> <label for="rad2">Today FM</label>
</div>

<div>
  <input type="radio" name="station" id="rad3" value="abc-news"/> <label for="rad3">ABC News</label>
</div>

<div>
  <input type="radio" name="station" id="rad4" value="triple-j"/> <label for="rad4">Triple J</label>
</div>
```

A very important thing to note is that, while the name attribute has the same value in each case, the value attribute differs. As the user does not actually enter any text into a radio button (that's clearly impossible), there must be a way to assign a meaning to each.

Unlike the name attribute, the id attribute should be unique. Here, the label element, through its for attribute, relates itself to the input it is labeling. We will look at the label element again at the end of this section.

The *textarea* Element

The textarea element is similar to the text input, but it allows the user to enter multiple lines of text, as opposed to a single line of text. This makes it ideal for larger amounts of text. Unlike the input element, a textarea element has an opening <textarea> and closing </textarea> tag in which only text content is allowed.

```
<textarea name="description"></textarea>
```

It's easy to change the size of a textarea element by making use of the cols and rows attributes, which, as you might imagine, specify the number of horizontal input lines (rows) and the width of the textarea in terms of columns.

```
<textarea name="description" rows="4" cols="50" ></textarea>
```

The *select* Element

The select element is a container for a series of option elements. These option elements display in the browser as a drop-down list. Unless you use the multiple attribute, this control will allow the user to pick just one item from the list of options. Take a look at Listing 6-2, which shows two select elements, one with the multiple attribute specified and one without it specified.

Listing 6-2. Two Very Similar select elements, Two Very Different Outcomes

```
<!-- this renders as a drop down lst -->
<select name="favorite-food" id="favorite-food">
    <option>Eggs</option>
    <option>Fish</option>
    <option>Bread</option>
</select>

<!-- this renders as a all-in-one list -->
<select name="favorite-food" id="favorite-food" multiple >
    <option>Eggs</option>
    <option>Fish</option>
    <option>Bread</option>
</select>
```

These are close to identical. The only difference is that the second select element uses the multiple attribute. Figure 6-1 shows the rendered lists.

Figure 6-1. Lists with and without the multiple attribute

It is common to see the select element set up such that its first option is the user's prompt. For example, the select element in Listing 6-3 uses its first option to display "Choose your favorite food."

Listing 6-3. Using the First option Element As a Prompt

```
<select name="favorite-food" id="favorite-food">
    <option value="">Choose your favorite food</option>
    <option value="eggs">I love Eggs!</option>
    <option value="fish">Fish is my fave!</option>
    <option value="bread">Bread rocks!</option>
</select>
```

An important point to observe about Listing 6-3 is that it uses the value attribute. If the user were to select the option "I love eggs!", the value submitted to the server would be "eggs." The option used as the prompt has an empty string as its value. This is simply a way to signify the fact that this option isn't really an actual choice; it's merely serving as an instruction to the user.

There is certainly more to the select element, and indeed forms in general, but I hope this section has given you a brief introduction (or perhaps rehydrated some knowledge that was perilously close to drying up and disappearing for good!).

The *label* Element

The label element defines a label for an input element. This element provides a usability improvement, because it creates a connection to the input to which it refers. So, for example, screen readers can better distinguish that the text you provide as a label is related to the input field. An additional benefit is that the label will also help users target the input with which it is associated, so check boxes and radio buttons are much easier to click, as they can now be activated by clicking the label itself.

In the example that follows, you can see that this connection is made by specifying a value on the for attribute that matches the value of the input's id attribute. In this case, first-name is used in both cases.

```
<label for="first-name">Enter Your First Name</label>
<input type="text" name="first-name" id="first-name" size="20"/>
```

Here is another example, this time using a check box.

```
<label for="terms">I agree to the terms and conditions</label>
<input type="checkbox" name="terms" id="terms" value="agree">
```

Simply by clicking the text "*I agree to the terms and conditions*" can activate this check box. Had we not used a label and instead opted to use some other element, such as a p or a div, users would have to click the check box itself.

Model Binding

When we speak about *binding,* we are really just talking about connecting things in such a way that they remain in sync with each other. What *things* are we talking about here? For example, we can bind a model property called firstName to a text input. This binding would create a special relationship between each, causing the text input to display the value of the model property, and the model property to store the value of the text input.

It's even more than that, however, because it works in both directions and in near real time. Should you change the value in the text input, the model property will immediately update itself to reflect this new value. Should you change the value of the model property, the value in the text input will immediately update itself to display this new value. As this all happens in near real time, changes are visible in the user interface right away.

■ **Note** AngularJS model binding happens inside a process called the *digest loop*. In simple terms, the digest loop is triggered whenever a change is detected in the values that AngularJS is watching. I use the term *near real time* here, because this process, despite how fast it is, is technically not in "real time." There are advanced-use cases for which this subtlety matters.

How do we set up a binding between a model property, such as firstName, and a text input? Well, it's surprisingly easy, thanks to the ngModel directive.

```
<input type="text" name="firstName" ng-model="firstName"/>
```

Here, we use the ngModel directive on the input to define a two-way binding. Because we specified firstName as the value of the ngModel directive, we connected it to the model property of the same name. A very important aspect of this process is the fact that it all happens against the current scope. In this particular (and common) scenario, it would be the scope object used in your controller. When firstName was bound to the text input, it was actually $scope.firstName that was bound. As discussed earlier in the book, the scope reference is implicit within AngularJS expressions.

Let's look at Listing 6-4 and see some model binding in action. Here is the controller code:

Listing 6-4. Setting Some Model Properties on the Scope

```
angular.module("myapp", [])
.controller("MyController", function ($scope) {

  var person = {
    firstName:"Jimmy",
    age: 21,
    address:{
      street: '16 Somewhere Drive',
      suburb: 'Port Kennedy',
      state:  'Western Australia'
    }
  }

  $scope.person = person;

});
```

Now let's look at Listing 6-5, which shows a portion of HTML code that uses this controller and model.

Listing 6-5. ngModel in Action

```
<div ng-app="myapp">

  <div ng-controller="MyController">

    <form name="theForm">
      <input type="text" name="firstName" ng-model="person.firstName"/><br/>
      <input type="text" name="firstName" ng-model="person.address.street"/>
    </form>
```

```
    <p>
      First name is:  {{person.firstName}} <br/>
      Street name is: {{person.address.street}}
    </p>

  </div>
</div>
```

Listing 6-4 and Listing 6-5 show the general principles of binding in action. Pay special attention to the fact that we bound to a model property with a nested object (the person object's address property, which is itself an object). Both text inputs properly reflect this hierarchy, as shown in bold in the code listing.

More formally, what I have been discussing in this section is known as *two-way binding*. This distinction is made because AngularJS also supports one-way binding. You have already used one-way binding, and it is used in Listing 6-5. Here is the portion of code in which the one-way binding appears:

```
First name is:  {{person.firstName}} <br/>
Street name is: {{person.address.street}}
```

We have already seen this type of binding, though, at the time, we didn't actually use the term *one-way* binding. What exactly do I mean by one-way binding? An easy way to understand this is by considering that a user cannot change a value that is output as plain text content. This is in stark contrast to values that are output to text inputs and other editable form elements. AngularJS has less work to do with the plain text output, as it does not have to manage the relationship in both directions. Consequently, this is called a one-way binding. AngularJS will not waste resources monitoring static content for changes.

In fact, as an alternative to using the double curly brace syntax, you can instead use the ngBind directive. The preceding code snippet, rewritten with ngBind, would look like this:

```
First name is:  <span ng-bind="person.firtName"></span> <br/>
Street name is: <span ng-bind=" person.address.street "></span>
```

The double-curly-brace approach is more naturally readable, and it requires less typing than the ngBind approach. However, ngBind can be useful, as it behaves like the ngCloak directive, discussed previously in the last chapter, in that content is only visible once AngularJS has loaded.

Here's a good thing to know about how AngularJS treats bindings in the absence of an associated model property: if you refer to a model property in an ngModel directive and it doesn't actually exist, AngularJS will create it for you. Review Listing 6-6 and Listing 6-7, and then we will have a quick discussion about what this reveals concerning the binding process.

Listing 6-6. Implict Model Binding—HTML Code

```
<div ng-app="myapp" ng-controller="MyController">
  <form name="theForm">
    <div>
      <input type="text" name="firstName" ng-model="firstName"> <br/>
      <input type="button" value="Show first name" ng-click="showFirstName()"/>
    </div>
  </form>
</div>
```

Here is the associated controller code:

Listing 6-7. Implict Model Binding—Controller Code

```
angular.module("myapp", [])
.controller("MyController", function ($scope) {

  $scope.showFirstName = function(){
    alert("Name is: " + $scope.firstName);
  }

});
```

Unlike in Listing 6-4 and Listing 6-5, the controller shown in Listing 6-7 does not create a model for our view template to use. However, as you can see in Listing 6-6, we clearly refer to a model property called firstName in the ngModel directive. Furthermore, we also show its value to the user when the Show first name button is pressed. How and when is the firstName model property created?

AngularJS created this model property for us when it came across the ngModel directive on the text input element. More accurately, it created it once it encountered a value to which it could bind. When the page first loads, you can click the Show first name button, and you will get the result shown in Figure 6-2.

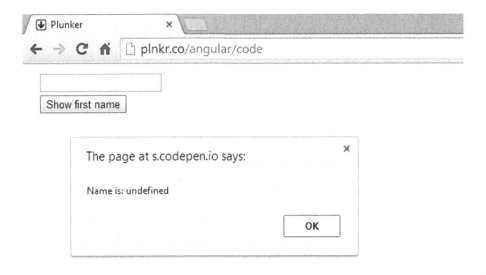

Figure 6-2. *An empty text input—nothing to bind to*

Perhaps, as you might expect, the value of firstName is displayed as undefined. Currently, there is no such model property, so this makes perfect sense. Now let's enter some text into the text input (see Figure 6-3).

Figure 6-3. *Text has been entered into the text input*

This time, the value of `firstName` is "Jimmy." As AngularJS is working in real time, once the text was input, it was able to create the binding. It's good to be aware of this behavior. Nonetheless, the fact that it can result in values such as `undefined` means that you should code defensively. This is demonstrated in Listing 6-8.

Listing 6-8. Coding Defensively

```
$scope.showFirstName = function(){
  if(angular.isDefined($scope.firstName)){
    alert("Name is: " + $scope.firstName);
  }else{
    alert("Name is empty, please enter a value");
  }

}
```

In Listing 6-8, we first test to see if the model property exists, and we only display it if it does. This listing uses the handy `angular.isDefined` method. In this version of the `showFirstName` function, the result of `angular.isDefined($scope.firstName)` will be true, even if you were to backspace and remove all of the text from the First name field. It will output an empty string as the value, although this is quite different from an undefined value. AngularJS has previously found a value in this text input; consequently, the binding and associated variable has been created and remains in play.

■ **Tip** `angular.isDefined` is just one of many handy utility methods that you can use. These methods can save you time and offer a standard approach to certain tasks. I encourage you to look them up in the documentation, which you can find here: `https://docs.angularjs.org/api/ng`.

With this knowledge of binding under our belts, let's now move on to using it to create forms. More specifically, we will create a small but, I hope, enlightening user registration form.

AngularJS Forms

With a discussion of standard forms and model binding behind us, we are in good shape to tackle AngularJS forms. Of course, AngularJS forms are really just regular forms enhanced with AngularJS goodness.

In this section, we will build a user registration form from scratch and employ it to build up our AngularJS skills. We will start off simple and enhance it along the way. Let's work with some very basic requirements for this form. These requirements are shown in Table 6-1.

Table 6-1. *User Registration Form Requirements*

Field Name	Data Type	Notes
First name	Text	Required
Last name	Text	Required
E-mail address	Text	Required
		Must be formatted as an e-mail address
Where did you hear about us?	Text One choice from a set of options: Television, Radio, Social Media, and Other	Must match the set of questions asked by Marketing across the various communication channels
Would you like to subscribe to our quarterly newsletter?	Yes or no	Must be unchecked by default
Register	Text	The text that appears on the submit button

■ **Tip**   The more information and detail you can get before coding even a simple form, the easier the testing and quality-control process will be later!

It's fairly clear from these requirements, in general terms, at least, what we will need to build, in terms of a user interface. Let's take a look at some first-draft HTML code (Listing 6-9) that reflects something close to what we are targeting.

Listing 6-9. First-Draft HTML Code for a User Registration Form

```
<div ng-app="myapp" ng-controller="MyController">
  <form name="registrationForm">

    <input type="text" placeholder="First Name" name="firstName" ng-model="person.firstName" required>
    <br/>

    <input type="text" placeholder="Last Name" name="lastName" ng-model="person.lastName" required>
    <br/>
```

```
<input type="email" placeholder="Email" name="email" ng-model="person.email" required>
<br/>

<select name="channels" ng-model="person.channels"
  <option value="">Where did you hear about us?</option>
</select>
<br/>

<input ng-model="person.newsletterOptIn" type="checkbox" name="newsletterOptIn"
       id="newsletterOptIn" value="newsletterOptIn"/>
<label for="newsletterOptIn">Recieve monthly
  newsletter</label>
<br/>

<input type="submit" value="Register">

  </form>
</div>
```

For the most part, this is straightforward HTML. The two most important things to note are the existence of the ngModel directive on each of the form elements and the fact that we have given the form a name. Giving the form a name means that we can access some interesting AngularJS features, which I will discuss shortly. This form does not yet meet the requirements, but we are well on the way. Figure 6-4 reveals how the form looks right now.

Figure 6-4. *First-draft user registration form*

It's far from perfect, but we are on the right track. Let's work our way through each of the fields, starting with the First name and Last name fields (which are the same in terms of the requirements). Take note that both of these fields make use of the required attribute. This attribute, which is an HTML5 attribute, not an AngularJS construct, tells browsers to make sure that a value is entered before allowing the form to be submitted. I will talk more about this in the next section, which covers validation in more detail.

Let's move along to the Email field. This input element has a type of "email". This is very similar to a text input, but it is specifically used for capturing e-mail addresses.

```
<input type="email" placeholder="Email" name="email" ng-model="person.email" required>
```

This is not an AngularJS feature; it is part of the HTML5 specification. Compliant browsers will consider this field invalid if it does not contain a properly formatted e-mail address. I will touch on this point again in the upcoming validation section.

The Marketing team has asked us to include some research questions in our registration form. It wants to know among which set of communication channels the user has found our company. So far, we have created the appropriate form element, shown again in the code snippet that follows. However, we currently present just one option: the prompt for the user.

```
<select name="channels" ng-model="person.channels">
  <option value="">Where did you hear about us?</option>
</select>
```

This select element needs some AngularJS work, because the select element itself is only half the story. We have to turn to the controller, shown in Listing 6-10, whereby we can create some data for the list of options.

Listing 6-10. The Controller Code Driving the select Element

```
angular.module("myapp", [])
.controller("MyController", function ($scope) {

  $scope.person = {};

  $scope.person.channels = [
    { value: "television", label: "Television" },
    { value: "radio", label: "Radio" },
    { value: "social-media", label: "Social Media"},
    { value: "other", label: "Other"}
  ];

});
```

The controller, through the scope object, is making the person object available to our view template. More specifically, because our select element needs this data, it adds an array of objects to the model property we use on the select element's ngModel directive: person.channels. Another step is required, because we want the select element to be populated with a set of option elements, based on the model property we just added to the scope above. For this step, we use the ngOptions directive. Listing 6-11 shows the revised select element.

Listing 6-11. Using the ngOptions Directive to Generate Options

```
<select name="channels" ng-model="person.channels"
ng-options="obj.value as obj.label for obj in person.channels">
option value="">Where did you hear about us?</option>
</select>
```

The ngOptions directive expects a *comprehension expression*. This expression can seem a little intimidating when you first encounter it, but we can break it down. It is essentially a query that we use to tell AngularJS how to map our model property, the person.channels array, in this case, onto a set of HTML options. This array contains a set of objects, and AngularJS would like to know which properties of this set should become the option element's value and which should become the content visible to our end user. Here is the expression again:

obj.**value** as obj.**label** for obj in **person.channels**

It isn't a particularly intuitive syntax, but we can make out the key components. In plain English, this would read something like the following:

Use the value property on the option elements value attribute, and use the label property as the text displayed within the option element. Oh, and by the way, I am referring to the objects contained within the person.channels array.

■ **Tip**   In AngularJS terminology, this kind of expression is known as a *comprehension expression*. It is used to create a data source for the ngSelect directive from an object or an array. You can find out more in the online documentation at https://docs.angularjs.org/api/ng/directive/select.

While we used the ngOptions directive to generate the option elements, we added the Where did you hear about us? option manually. Of course, you could add an extra object to the person.channels array representing this option too, but I prefer this approach, as it better reflects our ambitions about keeping things in the right place. This option element is just an instruction to the user, and it exists only to serve as part of our user interface; it isn't actually part of our model.

Next up, we have the "Would you like to subscribe to our quarterly newsletter?" question. As this requires a yes or no response, the checkbox element is well-suited to our needs. The only requirement that we have to address here is that the Marketing team wants this check box to be unchecked by default. We automatically meet this requirement, because check boxes are unchecked by default. However, we will set this explicitly through the binding we have set up on the check box. Here is the check box again:

```
<input ng-model="person.newsletterOptIn" type="checkbox" name="newsletterOptIn"
          id="newsletterOptIn" value="newsletterOptIn"/>
```

In our controller, we simply set the person.newsletterOptIn property to false. As this is used as a binding, the check box, fully aware of the need to check and uncheck itself in response to true and false values, automatically takes on the correct value. Had we wanted the check box to appear checked, we could have set this value to true instead, which would have caused the check box to appear checked. Of course, it is not a good practice to put the onus on the user to opt out, so we won't do that. Listing 6-12 shows this in action.

Listing 6-12. The Controller Code Driving the Check Box

```
angular.module("myapp", [])
.controller("MyController", function ($scope) {

  $scope.person = {};
  $scope.person.newsletterOptIn = false;

  $scope.person.channels = [
    { value: "television", label: "Television" },
    { value: "radio", label: "Radio" },
    { value: "social-media", label: "Social Media"},
    { value: "other", label: "Other"}
  ];

});
```

This approach is not quite as easy as adding the checked attribute to the HTML code, but it's not too much extra effort. I chose this approach because it better showcases bindings in action. However, it also has benefits in other scenarios, such as when you have to populate forms with existing data (as with forms that users can come back and update at a later time).

The last form element is the submit button. The only thing we have done so far is to change its value to "register", as opposed to leaving it with the default "Submit" value. The Marketing team has yet to tell us how we should handle this data with regard to what should happen when a user registers, but I suspect it will have filled us in on this just in time for the next chapter. For now, though, we can attach a submit handler to our form, so that it is ready to handle this pending requirement. Here is the revised form element:

```
<form name="registrationForm" ng-submit="person.register()">
```

By using the ngSubmit directive, we have told the form to use a method on our person object (the register() method) when the user submits the form. The revised controller code is shown in Listing 6-13.

Listing 6-13. Adding the submit Handler

```
angular.module("myapp", [])
.controller("MyController", function ($scope) {

  $scope.person = {};
  $scope.person.newsletterOptIn = false;

  $scope.person.channels = [
    { value: "television", label: "Television" },
    { value: "radio", label: "Radio" },
    { value: "social-media", label: "Social Media"},
    { value: "other", label: "Other"}
  ];

  $scope.person.register = function () {
      <!-- pending implementation -->
  }

});
```

We are closer to fulfilling the requirements, but there is still work to be done. Before we move on to the topic of validation, it's time for a checkpoint. Listing 6-14 shows the HTML code, and Listing 6-15 shows the slightly refactored JavaScript code.

Listing 6-14. The Form Code

```
<div ng-app="myapp" ng-controller="MyController">

  <form name="registrationForm" ng-submit="person.register()">

    <input type="text" placeholder="First Name" name="firstName" ng-model="person.firstName" required>
    <br/>

    <input type="text" placeholder="Last Name" name="lastName" ng-model="person.lastName" required>
    <br/>

    <input type="email" placeholder="Email" name="email" ng-model="person.email" required>
    <br/>
```

```
  <select name="level" ng-model="person.levels"
          ng-options="obj.label as obj.value for obj in person.channels">
    <option value="">Where did you hear about us?</option>
  </select>
  <br/>

  <input ng-model="person.newsletterOptIn" type="checkbox" name="newsletterOptIn"
         id="newsletterOptIn" value="newsletterOptIn"/>
  <label for="newsletterOptIn">Recieve monthly
    newsletter</label>

  <br/>

  <input type="submit" value="Register" ng-click="person.register()">

</form>
</div>
```

The only change in the JavaScript code in Listing 6-15 is that the person object is constructed first and then assigned to the $scope as the last step. The end result is the same, but this is much more readable.

Listing 6-15. The AngularJS Code

```
angular.module("myapp", [])
.controller("MyController", function ($scope) {

    var person = {};
    person.newsletterOptIn = false;
    person.channels = [
      { value: "television", label: "Television" },
      { value: "radio", label: "Radio" },
      { value: "social-media", label: "Social Media"},
      { value: "other", label: "Other"}
    ];
    person.register = function () {
      <!-- pending implementation -->
    }

});
```

Validating Forms

We usually want to validate at least some of the data that users enter into our forms. While it is true that validation can and should be done on the server, and that server-side processes are usually capable of handling much more complex validation rules, we still have to perform *first-line-of-defense* validation in the web browser. With JavaScript validation, we can do a lot of the validation up front, before even considering sending it along to the server. This way, we preserve bandwidth and reduce the load placed on our web servers. The fact that JavaScript validation provides instant feedback is a big plus too.

Using AngularJS, it isn't difficult or terribly time-consuming to implement JavaScript validation. The first step has already been taken with our registration form: when we gave the form a name, we enabled access to AngularJS validation features.

Before we look at validation as it applies to specific fields, let's look at what AngularJS does for us in regard to the form as a whole. At this *form-wide* level, AngularJS will give us answers to some important questions: Has the user started entering any data into the form yet? Is the form as a whole in a valid state? and so on.

Answers to questions such as these are useful in a lot of situations. You will see an example in our registration form's validation, as we will determine whether or not to allow the form to submit, based on whether or not the form is completely valid. We can do such things because AngularJS exposes the answer to these questions via a set of built-in form properties, as shown in Table 6-2.

Table 6-2. *Built-in Form-Level Properties*

Property Name	Description
$pristine	True, if user has not yet interacted with the form
$dirty	True, if user has already interacted with the form
$valid	True, if all of the containing forms and form elements are valid
$invalid	True, if at least one containing form element or form is invalid

We also have access to some very handy CSS style hooks. As the form changes state, such as when it moves from valid to invalid, AngularJS will dynamically add and remove CSS classes to reflect the current state. You can create your own set of CSS rules for these classes, thereby styling the form as you see fit for each state. These classes are outlined in Table 6-3. The style hooks and the built-in form properties will make more sense when we see them in action.

Table 6-3. *Dynamically Managed Validation Classes*

Class	Description
ng-valid	Set, if the form is valid
ng-invalid	Set, if the form is invalid
ng-pristine	Set if the form is pristine
ng-dirty	Set, if the form is dirty
ng-submitted	Set, if the form was submitted

If you have already worked with the HTML5 specification, you might be pleased to hear that AngularJS respects attributes such as type and required. It also adds some directives of its own to support forms and form validation further. Generally, one of the first steps you take when using AngularJS validation is the addition of the novalidate attribute on your form element, as shown here:

```
<form name="registrationForm" ng-submit="person.register()" novalidate>
```

Strange that we should use the novalidate attribute when we actually want to validate. Keep in mind that the novalidate attribute is not an AngularJS directive; it is a standard HTML attribute that is used to prevent built-in browser validation. The reason we use it is because we want AngularJS to validate our form. Taking the built-in browser behavior out of the equation is the best way to remedy the problems that would otherwise occur. We still get to use the same approach, only with AngularJS running the show instead of the browser.

As we have given our form a name and we have added the novalidation attribute, it is now primed for validation. Let's look at validation for the First name and Last name fields. These won't be too challenging, as the rule is simply that they are required. The two things that we must do are provide the validation itself and the feedback to the user, if the validation fails. Examine Listing 6-16.

Listing 6-16. Validating Required Fields and Showing Feedback to the User

```
<input type="text" placeholder="First Name" name="firstName" ng-model="person.firstName" required>
<span ng-show="firstNameInvalid">Please enter a value for First name</span>
<br/>

<input type="text" placeholder="Last Name" name="lastName" ng-model="person.lastName" required>
<span ng-show="lastNameInvalid">Please enter a value for Last name</span>
```

The validation is straightforward; we simply add a required attribute to our input elements. With the addition of this attribute, AngularJS will insist on a value in each of these fields before it will consider the form valid. However, it insists rather quietly, so it is up to us to tell the user if things went wrong and how to fix them. The approach we apply here is to use span elements containing the validation error messages. We want to keep these hidden until we have to show them. We achieve this through the ngShow directive. Let's focus on the span we added for the First name field.

```
<span ng-show="firstNameInvalid">Please enter a value for First name</span>
```

As you may recall from our coverage of ngShow in the last chapter, it expects an expression that evaluates to a Boolean value. Let's turn to the controller code's register method in Listing 6-17, as this will show us how the firstNameInvalid variable is manipulated to trigger the showing and hiding of the validation message.

Listing 6-17. The Registration Method with Some Validation in Place

```
$scope.register = function () {

  $scope.firstNameInvalid = false;
  $scope.lastNameInvalid = false;

  if(!$scope.registrationForm.firstName.$valid){
    $scope.firstNameInvalid = true;
  }

  if(!$scope.registrationForm.lastName.$valid){
    $scope.lastNameInvalid = true;
  }

  if($scope.registrationForm.$valid){
      <!-- pending implementation -->
  }

}
```

When the document first loads, both firstNameInvalid and lastNameInvalid evaluate to false. Consequently, the ngShow directives will keep the span elements, and therefore the validation messages, hidden. When the user presses the submit button, we make use of the fact that AngularJS can tell us, on a field-by-field basis, whether or not an input is valid. In the case of the First name field, which we named firstName, in the form which we named registrationForm, we can use $scope.registrationForm.firstName.$valid to see if this field is currently valid. As you might expect, this scope.formName.fieldName.$property format applies to the Last name field too.

Both of the conditional statements in the register() method work the same way; they each check to see if these fields are *not* currently valid. If indeed they are not, then the firstNameInvalid and lastNameInvalid variables are set to true. This will cause the ngShow directive to show the validation error messages.

Moving along to the e-mail address input, the requirement is also that the field is required. In this case, it must also be a value that is a properly formatted e-mail address. This is easy enough to achieve using the HTML5-based approach. Study the following input element, which will achieve this:

```
<input type="email" placeholder="Email" name="email" ng-model="person.email" required>
```

■ **Note**   As we did before, we again use the **required** attribute. In this case, we also make use of one of the HTML5-based input types and specify email as the input type. This means that only properly formatted e-mail addresses will be considered valid. As you will see shortly, we can take exactly the same approach as we did with the First name and Last name fields and use the ngShow directive to show and hide the associated validation error message. The same applies to the research questions' select element.

■ **Caution**   I am often careful to say *"properly formatted -mail address,"* as opposed to saying *"valid e-mail address."* The two are quite different things. The string x@xx.zx is formatted as an e-mail address, but it's not a valid e-mail address!

Let's use two more form-level properties that we touched on in Table 6-2. While this is a slightly contrived example, it does show off the use $pristine and $dirty.

At the top of our form, we will place two div elements; both of which use an ngShow directive. The $dirty property tells us if there has been some interaction with the form. It is true if at least some data has been entered. The $pristine property is the opposite. It tells us if there has been no interaction with the form. Only one of these div elements will be visible at any given time; that is, a form cannot possibly be in both states.

```
<div ng-show="registrationForm.$pristine">Form input has not yet started</div>
<div ng-show="registrationForm.$dirty">Form input has started</div>
```

Next, we will add a div element underneath our form. This div element contains the "Thank you" message that we want users to see once they have successfully completed the form. It, too, uses an ngShow directive. In this case, we rely on the value of the doShow variable, a variable that we set within the register() method of our controller, to determine whether or not to show the "Thank you" message.

```
<div ng-show="doShow">
  Thank you for taking the time to register!
</div>
```

I will show the complete code listing soon. Just one more thing that we should address before we finish up. At the moment, the form doesn't look too good. As Figure 6-4 shows, it's looking a little cramped and not very presentable. We will turn it into something a little better, as shown in Figure 6-5.

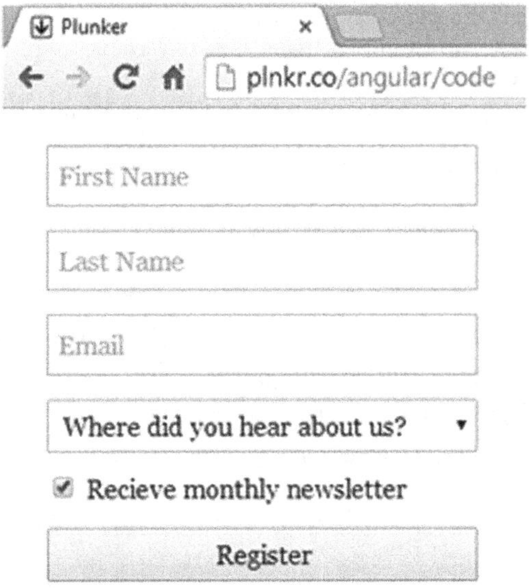

Figure 6-5. *Smartening up the form*

Thanks to a small amount of CSS, this looks a lot tidier. Most of the CSS, which is shown in Listing 6-18, relates to the look and feel of the form. However, I have also used a few of the AngularJS style hooks that I pointed out in Table 6-3. Here is the CSS code with the AngularJS style hooks shown in bold.

Listing 6-18. The CSS, Including the AngularJS-Style Hooks Behind the Form

```
body {
  font: normal 16px/1.4 Georgia;
}
input:not([type='checkbox']), select {
  width: 250px;
}
select, input {
  padding: 5px;
  margin-top: 12px;
  font-family: inherit;
}
input[type='submit'] {
  width: 264px;
}
form span {
  color: red;
}
input[name='email'].ng-dirty.ng-invalid {
  color: red;
}
```

```
input[name='email'].ng-dirty.ng-valid {
  color: green;
}
```

It isn't readily apparent what these last two CSS rules, the style hooks, accomplish, beyond the fact that they both set the CSS color property, one to red and the other to green. Figure 6-6 sheds some light on the matter. When the user begins to type, the input text appears in red, indicating that the e-mail address is not yet valid. Once the e-mail address is recognized as valid, the text becomes green. Figure 6-6 shows how this looks in both states.

Figure 6-6. *E-mail input, with visual real-time validation feedback*

What is particularly interesting about this feature is that it only requires the addition of some very basic CSS. As indicated earlier, AngularJS will dynamically add CSS classes as the form changes from one state to another. In this case, when the page first loads, the e-mail input element has a few classes set on it. One of them is the ngValid class. Here is how this particular input is enhanced by AngularJS upon page load:

```
<input type="email" placeholder="Email" name="email" ng-model="person.email" required=""
class="ng-pristine ng-invalid ng-invalid-required ng-valid-email">
```

Pay special attention to the two bolded classes, **ng-pristine** and **ng-invalid**. The former was added because this input has not yet been touched; it is in *pristine* condition. The latter was added because the field is currently invalid. Once the user starts typing his or her e-mail address, AngularJS will update this list of classes on the fly. At the very first keystroke, the input is no longer pristine. As the following code snippet shows, it is now *dirty*.

```
<input type="email" placeholder="Email" name="email" ng-model="person.email" required=""
class="ng-dirty ng-invalid ng-invalid-required ng-valid-email">
```

At this point, our input[name='email'].ng-dirty.ng-invalid rule kicks in, and the text becomes red. It remains red until such time as the e-mail address becomes valid. When it does become valid, the list of CSS classes is again revised by AngularJS.

```
<input type="email" placeholder="Email" name="email" ng-model="person.email" required=""
class="ng-dirty ng-valid-required ng-valid ng-valid-email">
```

This revision means that our input[name='email'].ng-dirty.ng-valid rule kicks in. Consequently, the text becomes green. This is quite a powerful technique, because once you know which classes AngularJS is adding and when, you can use these classes as hooks for just about anything you like. Of course, just because you can doesn't mean that you should! There was a little bit of legwork involved in building the validation and validation feedback code into our registration form, but it wasn't overly complicated. This has been a relatively long chapter, and I recommend that you load up this code in your web browser and favorite IDE; it is well worth doing some experimentation with it. The finished version can be found in Listing 6-19 and Listing 6-20. Admittedly, the validation rules that we studied here were fairly basic, but the general approach we used can take you quite far.

Listing 6-19. Registration Form—the HTML Code

```
<div ng-app="myapp" ng-controller="MyController">

  <div ng-show="registrationForm.$pristine">Form input has not yet started</div>
  <div ng-show="registrationForm.$dirty">Form input has started</div>

  <form name="registrationForm" ng-submit="register()" novalidate>

    <input type="text" placeholder="First Name" name="firstName" ng-model="person.firstName" required />
    <span ng-show="firstNameInvalid"><br/>Please enter a value for First name</span>
    <br/>

    <input type="text" placeholder="Last Name" name="lastName" ng-model="person.lastName" required />
    <span ng-show="lastNameInvalid"><br/>Please enter a value for Last name</span>
    <br/>

    <input type="email" placeholder="Email" name="email" ng-model="person.email" required />
     <span ng-show="emailInvalid"><br/>A valid email address is required</span>
    <br/>

    <select name="research" ng-model="person.levels"
            ng-options="obj.label as obj.value for obj in person.channels" required>
      <option value="">Where did you hear about us?</option>
    </select>
    <span ng-show="researchInvalid"><br/>Please tell us where you heard about us</span>
    <br/>

    <input ng-model="person.newsletterOptIn" type="checkbox" name="newsletterOptIn"
           id="newsletterOptIn" value="newsletterOptIn"/>
    <label for="newsletterOptIn">Recieve monthly newsletter</label>
    <br/>

    <input type="submit" value="Register"/>

  </form>

  <div ng-show="doShow">
    Thank you for taking the time to register!
  </div>

</div>
```

Here is the associated controller code:

Listing 6-20. Regsitration Form—the JavaScript Code

```javascript
angular.module("myapp", [])
.controller("MyController", function ($scope) {

  $scope.person = {};
  $scope.person.newsletterOptIn = false;
  $scope.person.channels = [
    { value: "television", label: "Television" },
    { value: "radio", label: "Radio" },
    { value: "social-media", label: "Social Media"},
    { value: "other", label: "Other"}
  ];

  $scope.register  = function () {

    $scope.firstNameInvalid = false;
    $scope.lastNameInvalid = false;
    $scope.emailInvalid = false;

    if(!$scope.registrationForm.firstName.$valid){
      $scope.firstNameInvalid = true;
    }

    if(!$scope.registrationForm.lastName.$valid){
      $scope.lastNameInvalid = true;
    }

    if(!$scope.registrationForm.email.$valid){
      $scope.emailInvalid = true;
    }

    if(!$scope.registrationForm.research.$valid){
      $scope.researchInvalid = true;
    }

    if($scope.registrationForm.$valid){
      <!-- pending implementation -->
      $scope.doShow = true;
    }

  }

});
```

Summary

In this chapter, I offered a brief introduction to HTML forms, and then we looked at how using JavaScript to enhance HTML form elements is much easier with AngularJS. We also looked at validation techniques and some interesting ways of providing validation feedback. By no means was this exhaustive coverage of working with forms in AngularJS, but I hope that this has given you a good overview, making you hungry to learn more.

Although we didn't actually do anything with the data captured by the form we created in this chapter, we will do so in the next chapter.

CHAPTER 7

Services and Server Communication

In the last chapter, we looked at HTML forms as a means of presenting a user interface for gathering a set of user registration data. However, we didn't look at the next step in the process, that is, sending that data along to a back-end server for processing. In this chapter, we will achieve this by using Angular services. As Angular services are about much more than sending data to servers, we will first look at them at a more general level.

The term *service* is rather overused in the development world, so what do we mean when we talk about Angular services? A good way to think about an Angular service is as a set of tightly related functions, managed by the Angular framework, which are made readily available for use across an application. For example, you might use something as common as a company-wide data service, which enables any part of your application to send and retrieve data to and from a corporate database. A marketing-and-communications-asset library, for example, which lets you locate and retrieve images and image metadata, is much more specific. When speaking of Angular services, however, examples such as these could fool anyone into thinking that services are all about server communication and data access, but they are not. In Angular, getting a reference to the browser's window object can also be achieved by using a service: the built-in $window service. You can even create animations by using the built-in $animate service.

If we wanted to, we could create our own JavaScript object and give it a set of methods that performs a range of related tasks. We could call upon this object whenever we needed it and, perhaps naively, describe it as a *service*. This seems to fit closely the description I just gave you of an Angular service, but not quite. So, what is it about an Angular service that makes it so special? While Angular ships with a set of very useful services, some of which we will look at shortly, the answer to this question lies in the fact that it provides us with a framework within which services can be easily managed. I say *easily managed*, because without this framework support, it wouldn't be a trivial task.

If you were to tackle a task like this on your own, and you were serious about it, you would (at a minimum) have to ask and answer the following questions:

- When and where is the right place to instantiate my service?

- What is the best way to manage service dependencies across my application?

- What is the best approach for making sure that my services can be unit-tested and configurable?

- How should I handle persisting and sharing services between my controllers?

Of course, the answer to questions such as these, and many more just like them, have already been addressed by the Angular team. As a developer, you need only learn some implementation details, but you can otherwise relax in the knowledge that you are using a solid and well-thought-out solution. That, to me anyway, makes Angular services pretty special.

Now that we know a little bit about what Angular services are at a high level, let's dive in and have a look at a few services that ship with Angular.

Using Services

As I mentioned before, Angular ships with a set of useful built-in services. We won't look at all of them in this chapter, but we will look at a few; just enough to get a sense of what is offered and how to put them into action.

The *$window* Service

The $window service is essentially a reference to the browser's window object. Access to the web browser's window object is globally available in JavaScript using the built-in window reference, but it is generally considered best practice to avoid it when using Angular, because it can cause testability issues. If instead we refer to it through the $window service, we keep our options open. For example, if we want to test our service in a non-browser context in which the browser's window object does not exist, we can more easily switch the underlying service provider to one that uses an alternate implementation, one which has all of the same properties and methods as the original.

Unfortunately, the use of service providers and advanced testing techniques is not covered in this book, but the real takeaway here is that, by using a service, we are creating an abstraction that shields us from being intimately tied to a specific implementation. The service simply does what we ask it to do, and users of the service don't have to worry too much about how it does this or even if it changes how it does this.

If you look through Listing 7-1, you will see that we access the $window service through the controller method's anonymous function. Here, we specify $scope as the first argument, as we have done on a number of occasions before, and then we *ask for* the $window service by specifying it here too.

Listing 7-1. The $window Service

```
<!DOCTYPE html >
<html ng-app="myapp">
<head>
    <title>Angular Services</title>
    <script src="js/angular.min.js"></script>
    <script>

        var module = angular.module('myapp', []);

        module.controller("MyController", function ($scope, $window) {
            $scope.winWidth = $window.innerWidth;
        });

    </script>
</head>
<body ng-controller="MyController">
        <p>Window width: {{winWidth}}px</p>
</body>
</html>
```

An important point here is that we didn't actually instantiate this service ourselves. The Angular dependency management sub-subsystem took care of that for us behind the scenes. This technique is an aspect of something known as *dependency injection*, a relatively involved topic that is beyond the scope of this book. For now, though, it is enough to know that *asking for* a service in this way, as opposed to you declaring and instantiating it yourself within your controller code, is a major benefit. That being said, you will get a little more insight into the mechanism at play here when we create our own service in the next section.

■ **Note**   Like other core Angular identifiers, built-in services always start with the $ symbol.

The idea of the window object as a service might seem a little odd at first, but it makes perfect sense. It contains a set of related functions and properties that we want to be readily available across our application. That's a service! Additionally, because it is a service, we don't have to be too concerned about how it goes about its work or how we might work with it in other contexts. While it may be early days in your Angular career right now, professional-grade testing is one such context you are likely to encounter in the future.

The *$location* Service

Based on the window.location object, the $location service parses the URL in the browser address bar and makes it available to your application. If you make changes to the URL in the address bar, they are reflected in the $location service, and if you make changes to the $location service, they are reflected in the browser address bar.

At first glance, it might seem like the $location service is merely a reference to the browser's window.location object, but it is a little more than this. It has tight integration with the Angular framework's life-cycle events, and it also has seamless support for the HTML5 history API (with automatic fallback support for older browsers). As a general rule, whenever your application needs to respond to a change in the current URL, or you want to change the current URL in the browser, this is the service to use.

■ **Caution**   The $location service will not cause a full-page reload when the browser URL is changed. In order to achieve this, you should use the $window.location.href property.

Listing 7-2 is a basic example of the $location service in action. Here, we use it to display the current URL and a list of URL parts.

Listing 7-2. Using the $location Service

```
<!DOCTYPE html >
<html ng-app="myapp">
<head>
    <title>Angular Services</title>
    <script src="js/angular.min.js"></script>
    <script>
        var module = angular.module('myapp', []);
        module.controller("MyController", function ($scope, $location) {
            $scope.url = $location.absUrl();
            $scope.protocol = $location.protocol();
            $scope.host = $location.host();
            $scope.port = $location.port();

        });
    </script>
</head>
```

```
<body ng-controller="MyController">
<p>The URL is: {{url}}</p>
<ul>
    <li>{{protocol}}</li>
    <li>{{host}}</li>
    <li>{{port}}</li>
</ul>
</body>
</html>
```

As we did with the $window service, we simply *asked for* the $location service by adding it as a parameter to our controller's anonymous function. In the next chapter, we look at how better to organize our HTML views, and you will see how the $location service plays a very important role in this context.

The *$document* Service

We will finish up this section with a brief look at the $document service. This service is essentially a jqLite (or jQuery) wrapper for the browser's window.document object. Examine Listing 7-3.

Listing 7-3. Using the $document Service to Access the Page Title

```
<!DOCTYPE html >
<html ng-app="myapp">
<head>
    <title>Angular Services</title>
    <script src="js/angular.min.js"></script>
    <script>
        var module = angular.module('myapp', []);

        module.controller("MyController", function ($scope, $document) {
            $scope.docTitle = $document[0].title;

        });
    </script>
</head>
<body ng-controller="MyController">
    <p>The page title is: {{docTitle}}</p>
</body>
</html>
```

Yet again, we ask for this service by specifying it as a parameter on our controller method's anonymous function. Next, we use it to get the value of the page's title element, and we set a property on the $scope, docTitle, on this value.

Angular generally discourages accessing the DOM directly, as it operates very much on the principle that a declarative approach is much better. There are times when you need this direct access, however, so it is good to have services such as this one available.

Why Use Services?

One thing that might have struck you as you read through these examples is that these particular services don't really add much in terms of functionality. The $window service, for example, doesn't appear to add much above and beyond what the regular JavaScript window object has to offer. While some Angular services, such as the $http and $animation services (which we will look at in later chapters), are very rich in functionality, what I want to convey in this section is that services are a core aspect of Angular and, regardless of what functionality a given service may offer, the way in which we access a service is consistent and offers important architectural benefits.

The $window service offers us the benefit of abstraction; we are not tied specifically to the browser's window object. So, in more advanced scenarios, we can actually switch it to use some other implementation. The $location service offers similar benefits, and it is also designed to work very well with the Angular routing framework (which we will also be looking at in a later chapter).

Angular services are an important part of how Angular applications are built, because they are a well-architected approach to managing dependencies, and they go a long way toward making applications much more robust. It shouldn't be too hard to start thinking in terms of services, because Angular uses them a lot. With a little time and experience, you will start to appreciate and realize the benefits of services, and you will develop a deeper understanding of where and when they should be used.

Creating Services

Angular services provide a mechanism for keeping data around for the lifetime of an application and for communicating across controllers in a consistent manner. As services are implemented as *singletons*, which are objects that are instantiated only once per application, you interact with the same instance of a service every time you use it. Angular is also performance-conscious, so it will create a service only when you need it and not a moment before. This is all great news, but it does mean that we must learn the ground rules when we create our own services.

We'll start off nice and easy with Listing 7-4. All that this service will do is to tell us the current date and the current time, but it's just enough to get an idea of how the plumbing works.

Listing 7-4. A Basic Angular Service

```
<!DOCTYPE html >
<html ng-app="myapp">
<head>
    <title>Angular Services</title>
    <script src="js/angular.min.js"></script>
    <script>
        var module = angular.module('myapp', []);

        module.factory('dateTimeService', function () {

            var dateTimeSvc = {};
            dateTimeSvc.getDate = function () {
                return new Date().toDateString();
            }

            dateTimeSvc.getTime = function () {
                return new Date().toTimeString();
            }
```

```
            return  dateTimeSvc;

    }).controller("MyController", function ($scope, dateTimeService) {

            $scope.theDate = dateTimeService.getDate();
            $scope.theTime = dateTimeService.getTime();

    });
</script>
</head>
<body ng-controller="MyController">

    <p>{{theDate}}</p>
    <p>{{theTime}}</p>

</body>
</html>
```

In Listing 7-4, you can see that we use the factory method on our module. This method takes two arguments, the first of which is the name of our service. We named this service dateTimeService. The second argument is the *factory function,* which returns an object. This object is known as the *service object,* and it represents the service that you will ultimately use in your application.

When the application first needs to use this service, the framework will call the factory function. In this example, the service object that it creates and returns is called dateTimeSvc, and it is this object that is used whenever the service is needed again. In other words, this service object, once created, is common to the entire application. This is a very important point, because it means that changes made to the state of this object remain in play throughout the lifetime of the application. We will see the implications of this later in the chapter.

As the primary purpose of our factory function is to create an object with our service's functionality, we busy ourselves doing just that. We set up an empty dateTimeSvc object, and then we attach to it the two service methods: getDate() and getTime(). We finish by specifying dateTimeSvc as the return value.

With the service in place, it's time to turn our attention to our controller, so that we can find out how to make use of it. The main thing to note about the controller function is that its second argument, the anonymous function, asks for the dateTimeService in exactly the same way that we have already seen when looking at the built-in services. As we registered our service using the name dateTimeService, Angular has no problem resolving this dependency for us.

Figure 7-1 shows the output of Listing 7-4. The result is simply two paragraphs containing the return values of the calls we made on our service.

Figure 7-1. The dateTimeService in action

It's a fairly bare-bones implementation of a service, but it does cover the basics of service creation. We will see these same principles and steps applied again shortly, but first, we will take a brief detour to look at a related aspect of our upcoming registration form submission task: the Promises API.

Promises

The JavaScript Promises API is an emerging standard, which has been implemented in major browsers. It's a relatively deep topic, but fortunately we don't have to dig very deep in order to start using it. Essentially, a *promise* represents a value that may not be available yet, but one that will be resolved at some point in future. This value is usually the outcome of an asynchronous task such as an Ajax call to a remote server, for instance, the Ajax call we will use to process our registration form data. Just like those we make to each other and to ourselves, a promise can exist in different states. To start, a promise is in a *pending* state. That is to say, a promise has been made, but that's about it. At some future point, it will become either a promise that has been kept or a promise that has been broken. In the Promises API, we refer to the former as a *fulfilled* promise and the latter as a *rejected* promise.

■ **Note**   A promise can only succeed or fail once. Furthermore, it cannot switch from fulfilled to rejected or vice versa.

The general idea is that you create callback functions and attach them to the different possible states of a promise. Figure 7-2 represents the general concept.

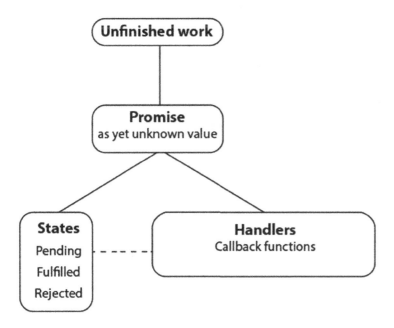

Figure 7-2. The role of a promise

The unfinished work represents the back-end processing and network communication that will take place once the user clicks our Register button. Both of these are processes that will take some time, but they will result in an outcome of some kind eventually. In the meantime, we have the promise, an object that represents this as yet unknown value. Furthermore, we have the ability to respond to the states of the promise, using callback functions.

The Promises API is very sophisticated, and it aims to improve on the way this kind of work was managed in the past. One interesting aspect of the API is the fact that you combine multiple promises into one larger promise. This is conceptually like promising your children a trip to the zoo, a toy from the toy store, and then some ice cream on the way home. With promises, you can write very clean and readable code that says, in essence, "When all of these things have happened, do this other thing." We won't get quite as involved as that in this book, but I do encourage you to dig deeper, if you plan to write a lot of potentially unwieldy asynchronous JavaScript code.

This is all a little abstract at the moment, but we are now ready to move on and look at server communication. Soon, we will see how our code can use promises.

Server Communication

While we don't have to concern ourselves too much with the back-end process that manages the incoming data, we do have to know how to transmit that data across the network. For this task, we are going to use the Angular $http service. This service allows you to communicate with a web server via the browser's XMLHttpRequest object. If you have a jQuery background, this service is similar to the jQuery Ajax method.

Take a look at Listing 7-5, some of which may make sense already, given our coverage of promises in the last section.

Listing 7-5. A First Look at the $http Service

```
var promise = $http({method: 'POST', url: 'memberservices/register', data: theData});

promise.success(function (data, status, headers, config, statusText) {
    // this callback will be called asynchronously
    // when the response is available
});

promise.error(function (data, status, headers, config, statusText) {
    // called asynchronously if an error occurs
    // or server returns response with an error status.
});
```

As Listing 7-5 shows, the $http service is a function that takes a single argument, a configuration object. While the configuration object lets you configure many different options, we keep it fairly simple here. We provide an HTTP endpoint via its url property, and we use the HTTP post method via the method property. We also use the data property to pass in the data that we want to send along to the web server. In many cases, this is all that the $http service needs in order to do its job. However, by using the configuration object, it is possible to configure a wide range of HTTP options as and when you need to do so.

We capture the return value of the $http service, a promise object, in a variable named promise. As a promise object is a representation of an event that can potentially have different outcomes, we use its success and error methods to cater to either possibility. Both of these methods accept callback functions as arguments, and each of these functions has the same signature.

```
function(data, status, headers, config, statusText) { }
```

The callback function arguments are outlined in Table 7-1. However, we will mainly be concerned with the first two, data and status, both of which we will see in action shortly.

Table 7-1. *The Arguments Provided to the Success and Error Functions*

Name	Type	Description
data	string|Object	The response body transformed with the transform functions
status	number	HTTP status code of the response
headers	function([headerName])	Header getter function
config	Object	The configuration object that was used to generate the request
statusText	string	HTTP status text of the response

Let's take the $http service and use it within our own service, a service we will call memberDataStoreService. We will use this new service to handle our registration form data, but this service could go on to perform other membership-related tasks, such as handling logins and the ability to change passwords. We will keep it simple here, though, and focus only on the registration. Take a look at Listing 7-6.

Listing 7-6. The memberDataStoreService Service

```
var module = angular.module('myapp', []);

module.factory('memberDataStoreService', function ($http) {

var memberDataStore = {};

memberDataStore.doRegistration = function (theData) {
                var promise = $http({method: 'POST', url: 'memberservices/register', data: theData});
        return promise;
}

return  memberDataStore;

});
```

There are a few things to note about Listing 7-6. We register our service using the name memberDataStoreService, and we make sure that our factory function has access to the $http service. Next, we create a memberDataStore object. This is to be the return value of our factory function and the object to which we can attach all of our service methods. As previously mentioned, we will limit it to just the one here, the doRegistration() method.

The doRegistration() method has just one argument: the data required to perform a registration. This is the data that is collected from the user via the registration form. Here's the interesting part: this method returns the promise object that was created by the call to the $http service. We very much want our service to take care of the connection to the web server and data transmission, but we very much do *not* want it poking its nose into our user-interface concerns. Using a promise, as you will see next, we can manipulate the user interface from within our controller code instead.

We are now ready to look at a more complete code listing. Listing 7-7 is a reworking of the registration form we built in the last chapter. This time, it makes use of our memberDataStoreService.

Listing 7-7. Making Use of Our Custom Service

```
<!DOCTYPE html>
<html ng-app="myapp">
<head lang="en">
    <meta charset="UTF-8">
    <title>Registration Form</title>
    <script src="js/angular.min.js"></script>
    <script>
        var module = angular.module('myapp', []);

        module.factory('memberDataStoreService', function ($http) {

            var memberDataStore = {};

            memberDataStore.doRegistration = function (theData) {
                var promise = $http({method: 'POST', url: 'memberservices/register', data: theData});
                return promise;
            }

            return  memberDataStore;

        }).controller("MyController", function ($scope, memberDataStoreService) {

            $scope.person = {};
            $scope.person.newsletterOptIn = true;
            $scope.person.channels = [
                { value: "television", label: "Television" },
                { value: "radio", label: "Radio" },
                { value: "social-media", label: "Social Media"},
                { value: "other", label: "Other"}
            ];

            $scope.register = function () {

                $scope.firstNameInvalid = false;
                $scope.lastNameInvalid = false;
                $scope.emailInvalid = false;
                $scope.researchInvalid = false;

                $scope.showSuccessMessage = false;
                $scope.showErrorMessage = false;

                if (!$scope.registrationForm.firstName.$valid) {
                    $scope.firstNameInvalid = true;
                }

                if (!$scope.registrationForm.lastName.$valid) {
                    $scope.lastNameInvalid = true;
                }
```

```
            if (!$scope.registrationForm.email.$valid) {
                $scope.emailInvalid = true;
            }

            if (!$scope.registrationForm.research.$valid) {
                $scope.researchInvalid = true;
            }

            // If the registration form is valid, use the
            // memberDataStoreService to submit the form data
            if ($scope.registrationForm.$valid) {

                var promise = memberDataStoreService.doRegistration($scope.person);

                promise.success(function (data, status) {
                    $scope.showSuccessMessage = true;
                });

                promise.error(function (data, status) {
                    $scope.showErrorMessage = true;
                });

                $scope.doShow = true;
            }

        }

    })

</script>

<style>
    body, input, select {
        font: normal 16px/1.4 Georgia;
    }

    input:not([type='checkbox']), select {
        width: 250px;
    }

    input, select {
        padding: 5px;
        margin-top: 12px;
    }

    input[name='email'].ng-dirty.ng-invalid-email {
        color: red;
    }
```

```
        input[name='email'].ng-dirty.ng-valid-email {
            color: green;
        }

        form span, .error {
            color: red;
        }

    </style>

</head>
<body>
<div>
    <div ng-controller="MyController">

        <form name="registrationForm" ng-submit="register()" novalidate>

            <div ng-show="showSuccessMessage">
                Thank you for taking the time to register!
            </div>

            <div class="error" ng-show="showErrorMessage">
                There appears to have been a problem with your registration.<br/>
            </div>

            <input type="text" placeholder="First Name" name="firstName" ng-model="person.firstName" required/>
            <span ng-show="firstNameInvalid"><br/>Please enter a value for First name</span>
            <br/>

            <input type="text" placeholder="Last Name" name="lastName" ng-model="person.lastName" required/>
            <span ng-show="lastNameInvalid"><br/>Please enter a value for Last name</span>
            <br/>

            <input type="email" placeholder="Email" name="email" ng-model="person.email" required/>
            <span ng-show="emailInvalid"><br/>A valid email address is required</span>
            <br/>

            <select name="research" ng-model="person.levels"
                    ng-options="obj.label as obj.value for obj in person.channels" required>
                <option value="">Where did you hear about us?</option>
            </select>
            <span ng-show="researchInvalid"><br/>Please tell us where you heard about us</span>
            <br/>

            <input ng-model="person.newsletterOptIn" type="checkbox" name="newsletterOptIn"
                    id="newsletterOptIn" value="newsletterOptIn"/>
            <label for="newsletterOptIn">Recieve monthly newsletter</label>
            <br/>
```

```
            <input type="submit" value="Register"/>

        </form>

    </div>
</div>
</body>
</html>
```

There is a fair bit going on here, much of which was covered in the previous chapter and some of it earlier in this chapter. However, pay particular attention to the code shown in bold. You will see that we now *ask for* the memberDataStore service when we set up our controller. Nearer to the end of the controller method, you will see the actual call to our new memberDataStoreService service. Following (Listing 7-8) is that section of code again:

Listing 7-8. Using the memberDataStoreService

```
// If the registration form is valid, use the
// memberDataStoreService to submit the form data
if ($scope.registrationForm.$valid) {

    var promise = memberDataStoreService.doRegistration($scope.person);

    promise.success(function (data, status) {
        $scope.showSuccessMessage = true;
    });

    promise.error(function (data, status) {
        $scope.showErrorMessage = true;
    });

    $scope.doShow = true;
}
```

There is no point submitting invalid data, so we first check to make sure that the user properly completed all of the required fields. Assuming that the user did, we can now send the data on its way, using the memberDataStoreService.doRegistration method. Note that the argument to this method is $scope.person. This contains the validated data captured during the form entry process.

Of course, this isn't the end of the process, as we still have to await the outcome of our attempt to submit the data. This attempt will either be successful or it will fail, and we cater to both possibilities, using the promise object's success and error methods. Both of these methods refer to some additional HTML elements that we have placed at the top of the HTML form. Following (Listing 7-9) is that section of code again:

Listing 7-9. Honing In on the Success and Error Messages

```
<div ng-show="showSuccessMessage">
    Thank you for taking the time to register!
</div>

<div class="error" ng-show="showErrorMessage">
    There appears to have been a problem with your registration.<br/>
</div>
```

Both of these div elements make use of the ngShow directive. Only one or the other will be displayed once the promise is resolved. The success method will set the showSuccessMessage to true or the error method will set the showErrorMessage to true.

What we have done so far is almost enough. However, we should enhance this to provide a slightly better user experience. Let's add a visual cue, so that the user is aware that some work is in progress once he/she clicks the Register button. The first thing we will do is to add a small loading animation next to our registration form's Register button.

The other thing we will do is use the ngDisabled directive on the Register button. The ngDisabled directive is very useful. If the value of its expression is true, it will set the disabled attribute on the element to which it is applied. Here, we use it to prevent the user from attempting to click the button more than once.

You can see these revisions in Listing 7-10 and Listing 7-11. Take note that the animation in Listing 7-10, a .gif image file, is inside a span whose visibility is determined by an ngShow directive.

Listing 7-10. Adding a Loading Animation and Disabling the Register Button

```
<input ng-disabled="working" type="submit" value="Register"/>
<span ng-show="working" style="padding-left:10px;">
    <img src="images/loading.gif"/>
</span>
```

Listing 7-11 shows the changes we have made to the register() function.

Listing 7-11. Indicating That Work Is in Progress

```
// If the registration form is valid, use the
// memberDataStoreService to submit the form data
if ($scope.registrationForm.$valid) {

    $scope.working = true;
    var promise = memberDataStoreService.doRegistration($scope.person);

    promise.success(function (data, status) {
        $scope.showSuccessMessage = true;
    });

    promise.error(function (data, status) {
        $scope.showErrorMessage = true;
    });

    promise.finally(function () {
        $scope.working = false;
    });

    $scope.doShow = true;
}
```

The first thing we do is to set $scope.working to true. So, thanks to ngShow, as soon as the user hits the Register button, the loading animation appears (see Figure 7-3). Of course, when the work is done, we want it to go away again. In order to achieve that, we simply set $scope.working to false. This also takes care of enabling and disabling the Register button.

Figure 7-3. Clicking on the Register button

We can't place this code in the success method, because, if an error occurs, our form will be trapped in its *working* state. This would lead to a somewhat conflicted user interface. We could put the code in both the success and error methods, however. That would work, though a much better way is to use the promise object's finally method. This is a cleaner way to handle this kind of task, the kind of task you want performed regardless of whether or not the promise was rejected or fulfilled.

■ **Tip**   No matter the outcome of a promise, the finally method will always be called.

Handling Returned Data

It is common for asynchronous communications to be a little more involved than simply sending data on its way. Some scenarios require us to process data with which the web server might respond. A username lookup service, for example, might require us to inspect a returned value to see if a given username exists within the system. How would we access this data? What about error handling? How do we find out if and what went wrong? We look at these considerations next.

Accessing Returned Data

It might be a simple transaction identifier or a large data set containing some or all of a customer's purchasing history; it doesn't really matter. Either way, this information, the server's response, is represented by the data argument with which we expect our success method's callback function to be supplied. Listing 7-12 shows how we might go about displaying a transaction number to our user.

Listing 7-12. Handling Request Data

```
promise.success(function (data, status) {

    $scope.successMessage = "Your transaction identifier is " + data.transactionID;
    $scope.showSuccessMessage = true;

});
```

This example assumes that we received a JSON response from the server and that this response was structured something like {"transactionID": "12587965"}. Of course, in your own projects, you will come across many different structures and even different formats, such as XML.

Handling Errors

It's an unfortunate fact of life that things do not always go well. Our applications are going to produce errors for a wide variety of reasons. Some might be network-related and quite possibly outside of our control. Others might be coding errors or configuration issues—things well within our control. Regardless of the origin of an error, we should respond appropriately. A good place to do so is in the promise object's error method (see Listing 7-13).

Listing 7-13. Handling Errors

```
promise.error(function (data, status) {

if (status === 0) {
    $scope.errorMessage = "network or http level issue";
} else {
    $scope.errorMessage = "response HTTP status is " + status;
}
    $scope.showErrorMessage = true;
});
```

This time, we make use of the status parameter. This will tell us how the server responded, by supplying us with an HTTP status code. Status codes between 200 and 299 are considered successful, so you won't see any in this range inside an error callback. If the server didn't respond at all, due to some kind of network or HTTP-level issue, you will get 0 as a result.

Listing 7-13 isn't a very sophisticated way to handle errors from a user perspective, but it is somewhat useful for "at a glance" debugging purposes. Ideally, though, you would evaluate your particular scenario and determine whether or not there is any way to recover from, or more gracefully handle, your own errors.

Summary

After looking at some of Angular's built-in services, we went on to develop our own custom service, learning a little bit about the $http service in the process. I hope you saw that while creating your own services may mean extra work, they aren't terribly difficult to create and are well worth the effort.

While directives get most of the Angular glory, I think that services are in some ways the slightly unsung hero. In this book, I really only scratched the surface of their possibilities and benefits, but, as you can see, they are a very capable way of isolating potentially complex logic from your model and view logic, and they are the ideal place for application-wide logic.

CHAPTER 8

Organizing Views

AngularJS excels when it comes to the creation of *single-page applications*, or *SPAs*, as they are commonly called. This kind of application has become increasingly common, given the advances in HTML5 and the availability of faster Internet connections. With an SPA, we can provide a much more responsive user experience, decrease the load on our web servers, and benefit from other advantages, such as the ability to cater better to users who might have to work offline. However, there is a potential issue with a web site or web application that downloads a lot of its content during a single-page request—organizing and managing that content.

With Angular, we can manage this situation neatly and easily, using the Angular routing system. As you will see, this approach makes for a very flexible and powerful solution to the problem of managing applications that are required to deliver large amounts of content (and functionality) in the context of a single-page application.

Ideally, we should be able to tell our application where our content resides, and, moreover, when users request it, it should just find it and load it for them with a minimum of fuss and complexity. This is where the Angular routing system comes into play.

By the end of this chapter, you should feel comfortable with the most important parts of the Angular system—the $route service and its related provider and directives. Before we look at any of this, however, we have to download and install the ngRoute module.

Installing the *ngRoute* Module

As the Angular routing system is defined within an optional module called ngRoute, we must download this module before we can get started. To do this, go to http://angularjs.org, click Download, select the version you require (the code listings in this chapter use the 1.2.5 version), and click the Browse additional modules link displayed next to Extras, as shown in Figure 8-1.

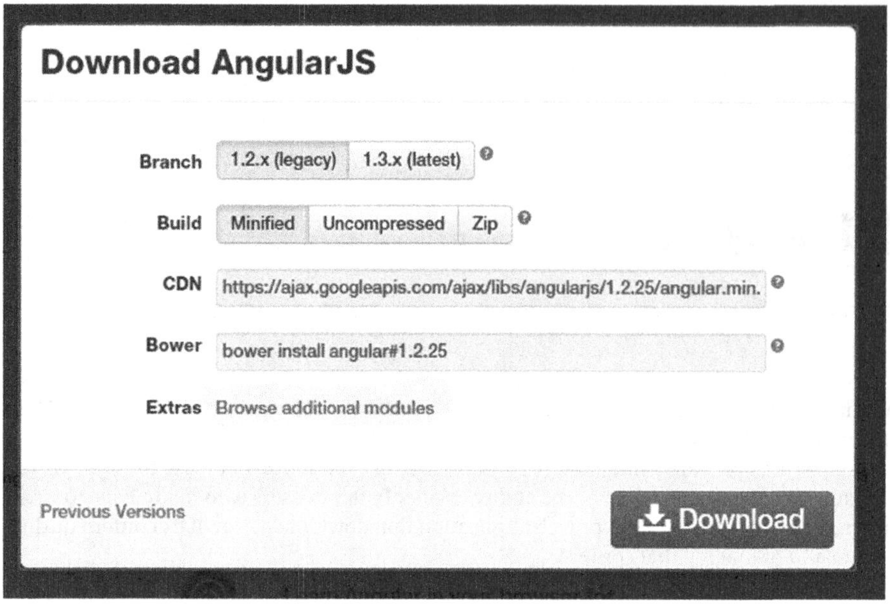

Figure 8-1. *Downloading additional modules*

A page listing various Angular modules appears. You want to download the `angular-route.js` file (or the minified version, `angular-route.min.js`, if you prefer) into your *angularjs* folder.

In Listing 8-1, you can see an example of how I added a script element for the `angular-route.js` file within a new HTML file.

Listing 8-1. Adding a Reference to the ngRoute Module

```
<!DOCTYPE html>
<html ng-app="myApp">
<head>
<title></title>
<script src="angular.js"></script>
<script src="angular-route.js"></script>
</head>
<body>
<!-- body code here -->
</body>
</html>
```

That's it—that's how you install the Angular routing system. Now let's start looking at what you can do with it.

■ **Note** Why is ngRoute defined in an optional module? Not every developer will want to use ngRoute, perhaps preferring to use another route system or no route system at all. In such cases, there is no point forcing users to download ngRoute if it is not going to be used.

Using URL Routes

You'll learn about routes through a small web site that we will create as we proceed through the chapter. Though it's a small web site, it will be more than able to demonstrate the power of the routing system. It will consist of a home page, an about page, and a contact page. In a traditional static HTML web site, we would structure this content as three separate HTML files, no doubt using the same navigation elements and other common features across each of the three pages. In this chapter, however, we are going to learn how to do something similar, but using the Angular routing system to *inject* these pages into a single container, or *parent*, view page.

Technically speaking, we could come up with a solution that does not require the use of the Angular routing system or learning anything new at all. For example, we could use ngShow and HTML div elements to manage the visibility of our content and rely on the use of $scope variables in our controller(s) to switch various pages on and off or perhaps load them on demand. There are other possibilities too, many of which revolve around the use of the versatile ngInclude directive. However, due to the added complexity and code required within controllers, these techniques can become cumbersome and increasingly difficult to manage as web sites get larger. What we really want is a clean and simple way to separate the task of selecting content from the controller, so that the application content can be driven from any part of the application. This is what routes allow us to do.

Defining Routes

At the heart of the routing system is the $route service. This service allows you to create a set of mappings between URLs and view file names. These mappings, usually known as URL routes or simply routes, work closely with the value returned by the $location.path() method. When this value changes such that it matches one of the routes, the corresponding view template (described by the route) will be loaded and displayed. Listing 8-2 shows a basic route.

Listing 8-2. A Simple Route

```
$routeProvider.when('/about',
                    {
                        templateUrl: 'pages/about.html',
                        controller: 'aboutController'
                    });
```

Don't worry too much if this code listing doesn't make total sense. This is just a first glance at what a route looks like. To begin, let's consider the purpose of the two arguments passed to the $routeProvider.when() method. The first is the path that we want the routing system to look for, and the second is an object that provides details of what it should do if it comes across it. These details, the template to load and the controller to use, are all that this particular route needs. Translating this code snippet into plain English, it might read something like this:

> When the URL has the path /about, load the view template /pages/about.html, using the aboutController.

Let's put some context around this with a more complete example. Listing 8-3 is the parent page of the small web site that we will be creating. This file, index.hmtl, is the entry point into the web site. The view templates, home.html, about.html, and contact.html, will be loaded into this page by the routing system as and when they are required. We will also have another view template, routeNoteFound.html, and this will be explained shortly.

Listing 8-3. index.html, the Entry Page for Our Demo Web Site

```html
<!DOCTYPE html>
<html ng-app="app">
<head>
    <link rel="stylesheet" href="//netdna.bootstrapcdn.com/bootstrap/3.0.0/css/bootstrap.min.css"/>
    <link rel="stylesheet" href="//netdna.bootstrapcdn.com/font-awesome/4.0.0/css/font-awesome.css"/>
    <script src="angular.min.js"></script>
    <script src="angular-route.js"></script>
    <script>
        var app = angular.module('app', ['ngRoute']);
        app.config(function ($routeProvider) {

            // configure the routes
            $routeProvider

                    .when('/', {
                      // route for the home page
                        templateUrl: 'pages/home.html',
                        controller: 'homeController'
                })
                    .when(' pages/about', {
                      // route for the about page
                        templateUrl: 'pages/about.html',
                        controller: 'aboutController'
                })
                    .when('pages/contact/', {
                      // route for the contact page
                        templateUrl: 'pages/contact.html',
                        controller: 'contactController'
                })
                    .otherwise({
                      // when all else fails
                        templateUrl: 'pages/routeNotFound.html',
                        controller: 'notFoundController'
                });
        });

        app.controller('homeController', function ($scope) {
            $scope.message = 'Welcome to my home page!';
        });

        app.controller('aboutController', function ($scope) {
            $scope.message = 'Find out more about me.';
        });

        app.controller('contactController', function ($scope) {
            $scope.message = 'Contact us!';
        });

        app.controller('notFoundController', function ($scope) {
```

```
                $scope.message = 'There seems to be a problem finding the page you wanted';
                $scope.attemptedPath = $location.path();
        });

    </script>
</head>
<body ng-controller="homeController">

<header>
    <nav class="navbar navbar-default">
        <div class="container">
            <div class="navbar-header">
                <a class="navbar-brand" href="/">My Website</a>
            </div>

            <ul class="nav navbar-nav navbar-right">
                <li><a href="#"><i class="fa fa-home"></i> Home</a></li>
                <li><a href="#about"><i class="fa fa-shield"></i> About</a></li>
                <li><a href="#contact"><i class="fa fa-comment"></i> Contact</a></li>
            </ul>
        </div>
    </nav>
</header>

<div id="main">
    <!-- this is where content will be injected -->
    <div ng-view></div>
</div>

</body>
</html>
```

We will come back to this code listing shortly, but for now, take note that we have made sure to add a script reference to the ngRoute module, and we have declared our dependency on it with the following line. Omitting either of these will result in a non-starter.

```
var app = angular.module('app', ['ngRoute']);
```

I used the Bootstrap framework to make this demo web site look presentable. Bootstrap is a popular front-end framework that contains HTML- and CSS-based design templates for typography, forms, buttons, navigation, and other interface components. Many web designers and developers find it indispensable, as it allows you to build great-looking web sites quickly. It is very easy to get started with Bootstrap. You can find out more at http://getbootstrap.com.

Figure 8-2 shows the result of my efforts on this demo web site. Each part of the web site has essentially the same look and feel, because the view templates, as you will soon see, ultimately become part of this single page. Factoring out these aspects of the code, all we really have here is the JavaScript code, which we will get to shortly, and a header containing some navigation links. What we don't see is any actual content. Near the end of the listing, however, we encounter the ngView directive. This directive is an important part of the routing system, and its job is to include the rendered template of the current route into the main layout file, which, in this case, is index.html. Every time the current route changes, the included view will change, based on how we have configured our routes.

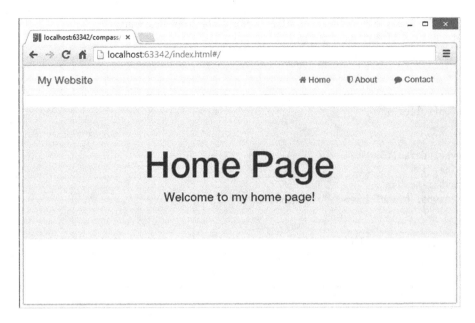

Figure 8-2. *Demo web site home page*

We have declared `ngView` as an attribute on a `div` element; consequently, this `div` element is where our content is going to be injected. Let's examine the four view templates that contain this content. These are shown in Listing 8-4, Listing 8-5, Listing 8-6, and Listing 8-7.

Listing 8-4. The HomePage, `home.html`

```
<div class="jumbotron text-center">
    <h1>Home Page</h1>

    <p>{{ message }}</p>

    <div>
    </div>
</div>
```

Listing 8-5. The About Page, `about.html`

```
<div class="jumbotron text-center">
    <h1>About Page</h1>

    <p>{{ message }}</p>

    <div>
    </div>
</div>
```

Listing 8-6. The Contact Page, `contact.html`

```
<div class="jumbotron text-center">
    <h1>Contact Page</h1>

    <p>{{ message }}</p>

    <div>
    </div>
</div>
```

Listing 8-7. The Route Not Found View Template, `routeNotFound.html`

```
<div class="jumbotron text-center">
    <h1>This is not good</h1>

    <p>{{message}}</p>
    <pclass="has-error">{{attemptedPath}}</p>

</div>
```

Each of these view templates will look the same, differing only in the content displayed once they are brought into the parent page via the `ngView` directive. Note the use of the `jumbotron` and `text-center` classes. These are Bootstrap-defined classes that help us with the layout. In the case of the `routeNotFound.html` view template, I have also used the Bootstrap `has-error` class to color the attempted path red, to highlight the erroneous input.

As I mentioned, every time the current route changes, the included view (the injected content) will change, based on how we have configured our routes. What would cause the current route to change? In our example, it would occur anytime our user interacted with the navigation links in our `index.html` file. So that we can hone in on these, I have repeated them again in Listing 8-8.

Listing 8-8. The Navigation Links in Our Entry Page, `index.html`

```
<ul class="nav navbar-nav navbar-right">
                <li><a href="#"><i class="fa fa-home"></i> Home</a></li>
                <li><a href="#about"><i class="fa fa-shield"></i> About</a></li>
                <li><a href="#contact"><i class="fa fa-comment"></i> Contact</a></li>
</ul>
```

You will notice that these links are declared using a # character, just like those used in HTML when addressing named anchors. By default, when specifying links for the routing system, you should use this style of link, because only the portion after the first # character is considered during the matching process. With this matching process in mind, let's have a look at some sample URLs and consider how the `$location` service can break them down into distinct components (see Table 8-1).

Table 8-1. *How the $location Service Works with URLs*

http://localhost:63342/index.html#/	
$location.path()	/
$location.url()	/
$location.absUrl()	http://localhost:63342/index.html#/
http://localhost:63342/index.html#/about	
$location.path()	/about
$location.url()	/about
$location.absUrl()	http://localhost:63342/index.html#/about
http://localhost:63342/index.html#/contact?someParam=someValue	
$location.path()	/contact
$location.url()	/contact?someParam=someValue
$location.absUrl()	http://localhost:63342/index.html#/ http://localhost:63342/index.html#/contact?someParam=someValue

Table 8-1 shows a few of the $location services methods acting on various URLs, though right now, we are mainly concerned with the path() method. It is this method that the routing system is using to determine whether or not the routes we configure are a match. Let's focus our attention back on index.html, or, more specifically, the route configuration we have in place. Listing 8-9 shows this portion of the file.

Listing 8-9. The index.html Route Configuration

```
var app = angular.module('app', ['ngRoute']);
  app.config(function ($routeProvider) {

    // configure the routes
    $routeProvider
            .when('/', {
                    // route for the home page
                    templateUrl: 'pages/home.html',
            controller: 'homeController'
        })
        .when('/pages/about', {
                    // route for the about page
                    templateUrl: 'pages/about.html',
            controller: 'aboutController'
        })
        .when('/pages/contact/', {
                    // route for the contact page
                    templateUrl: 'pages/contact.html',
            controller: 'contactController'
        })
```

```
            .otherwise({
                    // when all else fails
                    templateUrl: '/pages/routeNotFound.html',
                controller: 'notFoundController'
            });
  });
```

It is worth repeating the fact that we declared a dependency on the ngRoute module when we created our application module, because its absence is the source of many problems for Angular beginners. Next, we use our application module's config() method to set up our route configuration. While the config() method can be used for other configuration purposes, here we use it solely to set up the routing system. We do this using the $routeProvider parameter that we specified on its anonymous function argument. It is through the $routeProvider that we tell the routing system how we want it to behave.

■ **Caution** You may have noticed something unusual. We talk about the $route service, yet we use $routeProvider within the config() method. *Providers* are objects that create instances of services and expose configuration APIs. You need to use $routeProvider within the config() method, as this method is somewhat special. It can only use providers, not services.

The route provider's when() method adds a new route definition. As we discussed, this is achieved through the two arguments that we pass to it. In Listing 8-9, the first when() method is used to create a route for our home page. *When the routing system can make a match against the value of* location.path() *and* '/', *it will inject the template* 'home.html' *into the* ngView *directive and make* homeController *its controller.*

The next two route definitions use '/pages/about' and '/pages/contact', and the same logic applies. Of course, in these cases, the view templates and the controllers used are different. Pay special attention to the forward slashes in these routes. For example, the following two routes, '/pages/about' and 'pages/about', are not the same. Note that the latter is missing the forward slash. Without the forward slash, you run the risk of creating a Not Found error when navigating the web site. Keep in mind that the URL is evaluated relative to the value returned by the $location.path() method.

Sometimes, a match cannot be made. This is where the otherwise() method comes in. If you were to type a nonexistent URL into the browser's address bar, you would cause the otherwise() method to execute and display the 'routeNotFound.html' view template. Of course, only a single argument is required in this case, as a URL makes no sense in this context.

We also specified a controller to use with each of our route definitions. Listing 8-10 shows this again. All but the last one do nothing more than set a value $scope.message, so that we can distinguish one page from another.

Listing 8-10. The Controllers for Our View Templates

```
app.controller('homeController', function ($scope) {
     $scope.message = 'Welcome to my home page!';
  });

  app.controller('aboutController', function ($scope) {
     $scope.message = 'Find out more about me.';
  });

  app.controller('contactController', function ($scope) {
     $scope.message = 'Contact us!';
  });
```

139

```
app.controller('notFoundController', function ($scope) {
    $scope.message = 'There seems to be a problem finding the page you wanted';
    $scope.attemptedPath = $location.path();
```

You may have correctly surmised that the last controller complements our otherwise() route definition. Using $location.path(), this controller does something slightly more interesting; it sets a value for $scope.attemptedPath, so that we can display the invalid URL. This is the URL that could not be matched. Figure 8-3 shows how this looks.

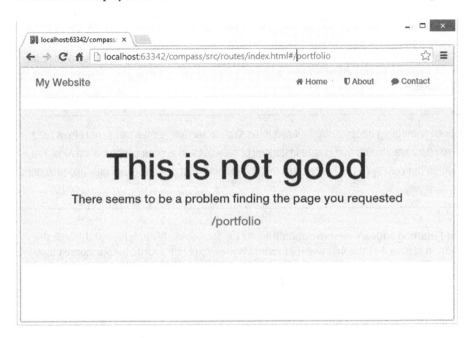

Figure 8-3. *The route not found screen*

If you load and view the index.html file at this stage, you will have a fully working, albeit minimal, web site. Take some time to follow the links back and forth, observing the structure of the URLs and entering random URLs to see the otherwise() method in action. Once you are ready, we will move on and build up your knowledge of the routing system further.

Route Parameters

The URLs we have used to define our routes so far have been relatively simple but somewhat inflexible. This is because the match against $location.path() has had to be exact. This is perfectly fine in many cases, but not when we want to add parameters to our URLs. Examine the following three route definitions.

```
$routeProvider.when("/product/123", { templateUrl: "product.html" });
$routeProvider.when("/product/789", { templateUrl: "product.html" });
$routeProvider.when("/product/926", { templateUrl: "product.html" });
```

All of these use a fictitious product catalog view template, product.html, but each has a slightly different URL. They each have a different series of numbers representing a product id. If we have 50 more products, each also represented by its own unique id, are we supposed to create 50 more route definitions? Of course not. Fortunately, we can deal with this situation, and others like it, using route parameters.

Route parameters are much more flexible than the fixed, or static, routes that we have seen so far. To demonstrate how they work, we are going to add a very simple contact form to our contact view template and use a route parameter to help us determine the initial state of its subject field. Here (Listing 8-11) is the revised contact view template:

Listing 8-11. The Revised Contact View Template

```
<div class="jumbotron text-center">
    <h1>Contact Page</h1>

    <form style="width:25%;margin:auto;" role="form">
        <div class="form-group">

            <input ng-model="subject" type="text" class="form-control" id="subject" placeholder="Subject">
        </div>
        <div class="form-group">
            <textarea class="form-control" id="message" placeholder="Message"></textarea>
        </div>
        <button type="submit" class="btn btn-default">Send Message</button>
    </form>

</div>
</div>
```

There's nothing too fancy going on here; it's just a basic form with two fields. We aren't really interested in submitting this form, so we won't pay any attention to the usual things (such as field validation and submitting it to a server). The important thing to take note of is the fact that we have a binding, named `subject`, in place on the subject field. The object of this exercise is to pre-populate the subject field, based on how the user ended up at this view template. This will make more sense when you look at Listing 8-12. This is the `about.html` file we saw earlier, but modified to support this feature.

Listing 8-12. The Revised About View Template

```
<div class="jumbotron text-center">
    <h1>About Page</h1>

    <p>If you want to learn more about us <a href="#/contact/learn">please let us know</a>.</p>

    <p>If you want a free quote give us a call or inquire through <a href="#/contact/quote">
    our contact form</a>.</p>
</div>
```

Again, there is nothing too fancy going on here, just a couple of paragraphs of content containing a couple of links. Take a close look at these links, though, as they contain our route parameters. Both of these links have two segments: the first one has the segments `contact` and `learn`, and the second one has the segments `contact` and `quote`. In both cases, the second segment acts as the route parameter under the route definition we examine next (Listing 8-13).

Listing 8-13. Additional Route Definition for the Contact View Template

```
// route for the contact page with subject param
    .when('/contact/:subject', {
        templateUrl: 'pages/contact.html',
        controller: 'contactController'
    });
```

The second segment in this route acts as a reference to whatever value is actually supplied as the second segment of a matching URL. Table 8-2 should shed some light on possible values for the subject route parameter, and it shows a couple of non-starters.

Table 8-2. *Possible Values for the subject Route Parameter*

URL	Match?
/contact/quote	Yes. The route parameters value is quote.
/contact/learn	Yes. The route parameters value is learn.
/contact/	Too few segments, no match
/contact/learn/more	Too many segments, no match

How can we do something useful with this? The first step is to extract the value of the route parameter. What we will use it for here is a simple comparison that will help us determine the text with which we want to pre-populate the subject text field. This is shown in Listing 8-14, which is a revision of the contactController code.

Listing 8-14. The Revised contactController

```
app.controller('contactController', function ($scope, $routeParams) {

var subject = '';
if ($routeParams ['subject'] == "learn") {
    subject = 'I want to learn more about your services';
} else if ($routeParams ['subject'] == "quote") {
    subject = 'I would like to get a free quote';
}

$scope.subject = subject;
        });
```

Extracting the value is easy, provided that we make the $routeParams service available to the controller, as we do here. We then create the variable subject, initializing it to an empty string. The conditional logic revolves around the value of the route parameter, and here you can see this value being retrieved via its name (also subject). Indexing into the $routeParams service in this way tells us the value that was actually used in the URL. As to how it got into the URL, let's look at the changes I made to the about.html view template (see Listing 8-15).

Listing 8-15. Creating URLs That Contain Route Parameter Values

```
<div class="jumbotron text-center">
    <h1>About Page</h1>
    <p>If you want to learn more about us <a href="#/contact/learn">please let us know</a>.</p>
    <p>If you want a free quote give us a call or inquire through <a href="#/contact/quote">
    our contact form</a>.</p>
</div>
```

Here you see the two links that will take us to the contact view template. Both /contact/learn and /contact/quote are a match for /contact/:subject. Of course, the route parameter subject is given a different value for each: learn for the former and quote for the latter. Listing 8-16 shows the new routes configuration.

Listing 8-16. The Revised Routes Configuration

```
app.config(function ($routeProvider) {

  // configure the routes
  $routeProvider

    // route for the home page
      .when('/', {
        templateUrl: 'pages/home.html',
        controller: 'homeController'
      })

    // route for the about page
      .when('/about', {
        templateUrl: 'pages/about.html',
        controller: 'aboutController'
      })

    // route for the contact page
      .when('/contact', {
        templateUrl: 'pages/contact.html',
        controller: 'contactController'
      })

    // route for the contact page with subject param
      .when('/contact/:subject', {
        templateUrl: 'pages/contact.html',
        controller: 'contactController'
      })

    // when all else fails
      .otherwise({
        templateUrl: 'pages/routeNotFound.html',
        controller: 'notFoundController'
      });
});
```

You can see that the new route definition is in play now. You can also see that the original route remains in play too. We still need this, so that we can continue to navigate to the contact view template *without* a route parameter. An alternative is to remove it and simply make sure that we always use a route parameter. It all depends on what you want to achieve. In this case, it made sense to leave it as a general purpose fallback.

Figure 8-4 and Figure 8-5 show the updated about.html and contact.html view templates. Figure 8-5 is the result of following the link in the second paragraph of the about.html view template. You will see that its subject field is pre-populated with the text *"I would like to get a free quote."*

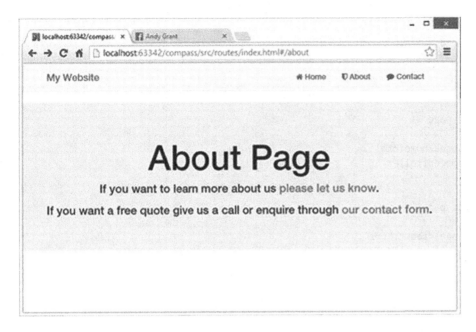

Figure 8-4. The updated about.html view template

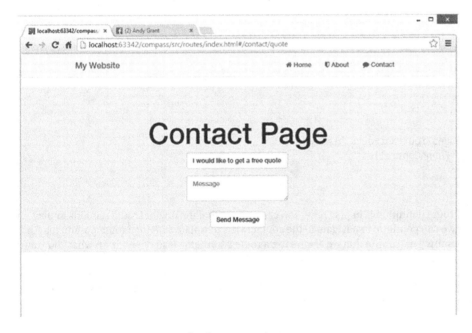

Figure 8-5. The updated contact.html view template

Eager vs. Conservative Routes

Routes such as `'/contact/:subject'` are known as *conservative routes*. That's really just a way of saying that the route would match, say, `'/contact/howareyou'` but would not match `'contact/how/are/you'`, as the latter has far too many URL segments. A conservative route is really quite strict about what it considers to be a match. To explain how an *eager* route works, let's start by considering a URL that contains segments that describe a product, more specifically, a shirt that is available in various sizes, styles, and colors.

```
/product/123/medium/blue/loosefit
/product/698/large/green/snugfit
```

Knowing what we already know, this is not a problem for us; we can use a conservative route. Such a route would look like this:

```
when('/product/:id/:size/:color/:fit', {
            templateUrl: 'pages/product.html',
            controller: 'productController'
        });
```

Inside our controller, we can do just as we did earlier and use $routeParams to access each value. $routeParams['color'] would give us the color, and $routeParams['size'] would give us the size, for example. However, this is still a conservative route. To match, it needs a URL with all five segments. With an eager route, you can do something like this:

```
when('/product/:id/:data*', {
            templateUrl: 'pages/product.html',
            controller: 'productController'
  });
```

Note that the use of the asterisk that suffixes the data parameter essentially says "match any path that has at least three segments, of which the first segment is product." The second segment will be assigned to the route parameter id, and the remaining segments will be assigned to the route parameter data.

■ **Tip** An eager route parameter is denoted by a colon, followed by a name, and then finally an asterisk. The key difference between an eager route parameter and a conservative route parameter is that the latter will match one segment, and the former will match as many segments as possible.

I personally haven't had a need to use this kind of route parameter before, but they can be useful in certain scenarios. For example, perhaps some shirts do not come with a slim-fit or loose-fit option, and perhaps some shirts have even more options. An eager route is flexible in such cases, as fewer or more options are simply fewer or more URL segments.

Route Configuration Options

We haven't looked at everything there is to know about the Angular routing system, though we've certainly reviewed enough to get you off to a good start. Before I finish this chapter, I'd like to leave you with a reference to some additional configuration options, as shown in Table 8-3, if only to give you a sense of what else is available.

Table 8-3. *Route Configuration Options*

Name	Description
controller	Specifies the name of a controller to be associated with the view displayed by the route
controllerAs	Specifies an alias to be used for the controller
template	Specifies the content of the view. (This can be expressed as a literal HTML string or as a function that returns the HTML.)
templateUrl	Specifies the URL of the view file to display when the route matches. (This can be expressed as a string or as a function that returns a string.)
resolve	Specifies a set of dependencies for the controller
redirectTo	Specifies a path to which the browser should be redirected when the route is matched. (This can be expressed as a string or a function.)
reloadOnSearch	When true (the default value), the route will reload only when the values returned by the $location search and hash methods change.
caseInsensitiveMatch	When true (the default value), routes are matched to URLs without considering case.

One particularly interesting alternative is the template option (see Listing 8-17). It's similar to the templateUrl option, but it differs in that it allows you to create the template right there in the route configuration options (as opposed to using a view template file). It's certainly not the way to do things in most cases, but it can be useful when you don't want or need a dedicated view template.

Listing 8-17. The Template Option

```
.otherwise({
    template: '<h1>Oops</h1>' +
              '<p>Sorry, page not found</p>'
});
```

Using template, Listing 8-17 shows this approach in action. As you can see, we do not specify a path; instead, we use a string value consisting of some HTML. As I mentioned, you generally would not want to use this approach unless you had a particular reason to apply it. The main reason I am presenting it here is to clarify the difference between template and templateURL.

As revealed in Table 8-3, besides accepting a string value, template and templateUrl can both accept a function as a value. This function must itself return a string. Both of the route definitions that follow are functionally equivalent.

```
when('/portfolio', {
    templateUrl: function () {return 'contact.html';},
    controller: 'contactController'
    });

when('/portfolio', {
    templateUrl: 'contact.html',
    controller: 'contactController'
    });
```

Of course, there's probably not much point in using the function-based alternative in this example. It's easier and much clearer to use the string-based approach. The real strength of the function-based approach is that it can be dynamic.

The example in Listing 8-18 does it much more justice. Here, we assume that we have ten portfolio pages, each one featuring a different piece of work. Each piece of work has its own view template, named `portfolio1.html`, `portfolio2.html`, `portfolio3.html`, all the way through to `portfolio10.html`.

Listing 8-18. A Dynamic `templateUrl` Value

```
when('/portfolio', {
    templateUrl: function () {
        // create a number between 1 and 10
        var num = Math.floor((Math.random() * 10) + 1);
        // use this number to produce a path
        // to one of the ten view templates
        return 'pages/portfolio' + num + '.html';
    },
    controller: 'contactController'
});
```

The function assigned to `templateUrl` is now a bit more interesting. This function creates a random number between 1 and 10, and it appends this number to the end of the file name. Each time the function runs, a different file name is created. Consequently, a potentially different portfolio view template is displayed each time.

HTML5 Mode

I made the point earlier in the chapter that, by default, links are declared using a # character. The # character is only there because we don't want the browser to fire off an actual HTTP request to the server. For example, if we removed it, a URL like the one following would create a request to the server.

```
http://mydomain/index.html/about
```

However, if we keep the # character as we do in the following URL, the browser will not fire off an HTTP request to the server, because the # character is telling it that we are seeking content on some part of the same page—the page that is currently loaded.

```
http://mydomain/index.html#/about
```

In reality, this whole approach is really just a workaround for non-HTML5 browsers. It works well, and it is perhaps the best approach to use if you are unsure who your target audience might be. However, a cleaner option exists. You can enable HTML mode. In this mode, the # character is not needed. A couple of reasons to do this might be that you want prettier URLs and much more SEO-friendly URLs.

Enabling HTML5 mode is not terribly difficult, but it does require some web server configuration and a relatively good understanding of how browsers and web servers handle links. I chose to remain in default mode, so as not to muddy the waters in this introductory book, but you should be aware of this option, and I encourage you to investigate further.

■ **Tip** Official coverage of HTML5 mode can be found at `https://docs.angularjs.org/guide/$location`.

Summary

Organizing your view templates isn't too difficult, but it can require some planning and familiarity with routes. You don't have to use the routing system, but if you want a clean and simple way to separate the task of selecting content from the controller so that the application content can be driven from any part of the application, it is a great option.

Of course, there are other factors to consider when organizing your view templates, such as how you name your files and how you structure your file system. Thus, you should consider the routing system as just one more powerful tool in your arsenal.

■ ■ ■

CHAPTER 9

AngularJS Animation

Animating your page element can be fun, but it can be easy to get carried away. Of course, you should only use animation to support your applications in a useful way. Subtly fading in messages or views, as opposed to having them appear abruptly, can be a useful and less jarring experience for the user, in some contexts. Perhaps you may wish to include a small scaling or transform effect to bring the user's attention to some event that has occurred—a file upload completing, for example. In this chapter, we will look at how to achieve such things. Ultimately, however, it is up to you whether to use your new powers for good or evil.

The $animate service is the one Angular uses to bring your applications to life, though, as you will soon see, you don't interact with this service directly. Instead, Angular uses CSS and some naming conventions to make things easier. Once you understand how this all works, you will be able to create a much richer user experience. However, if you aren't careful, you may also create a more annoying one!

Before we get started, we first must download the ngAnimate module. This is a very similar process to the one we followed to download the ngRoute module in the last chapter.

Installing the *ngAnimate* Module

Angular's animating capabilities reside within an optional module called ngAnimate, so we have to download this before we can get started. Just as we did when we needed the ngRoute module, go to http://angularjs.org, click Download, and select the version you require. (The code listings in this chapter use the 1.2.5 version.) Then click the Browse additional modules link displayed next to Extras, as shown in Figure 9-1.

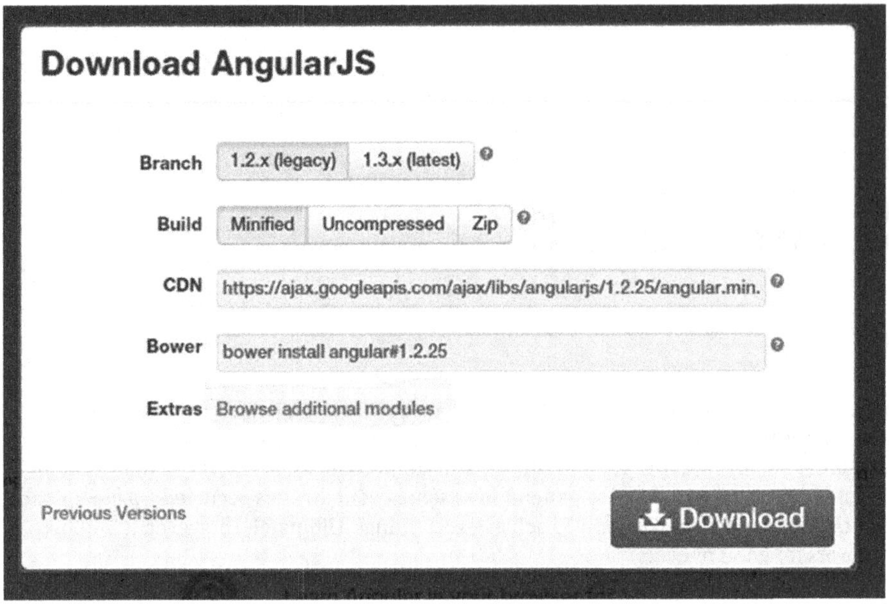

Figure 9-1. *Downloading additional modules*

A page listing various Angular modules appears. You want to download the `angular-animate.js` file (or the minified version, `angular-animate.min.js`, if you prefer) into your *angularjs* folder. Later in this chapter, in the "Applying Animations" section, you will see how to declare a dependency on this module.

CSS Animation Overview

It is possible to use JavaScript to create animations in Angular, but CSS is the preferred approach most of the time. Given the nature of the animations that are typically done in Angular applications, CSS is often the easier and more natural choice. Also, due to optimizations within most web browsers, CSS animation will also perform much better than JavaScript animation.

With this in mind, we will do a whirlwind tour of CSS3 animation capabilities before we look at how we can apply these skills in an Angular context. If you are already well-versed in CSS3, feel free to skip this section or use it as a brief recap.

CSS animation is a relatively large topic, and much of it resides in the newer CSS3 specification. A modern web browser is required to view most new animation features—something to keep in mind if you have users with older browsers. On the upside, animation tends to degrade gracefully in many situations. For example, an application that fades in a message would simply show that message suddenly, as opposed to fading it in gradually—hardly the end of the world. Obviously, if it's an issue for you, you should test your application, to be sure that it functions acceptably in such scenarios.

Speaking broadly, there are three main parts to CSS3 animation: transforms, transitions, and the more advanced Keyframe-based animation. They aren't mutually exclusive, and you certainly don't need to be an expert in all three to make good use of animation. We will look at transforms and transitions here, as they are the easiest to start with, and they will meet the majority of your needs when coding Angular apps. To begin, we will look at transforms.

Transforms

You can transform a web page element in several ways: you can rotate it, scale it, move it, or distort it along its horizontal and vertical axes (a process called skewing). Using a transform, you could, for example, make an image increase in size when a user mouses over it. You can even use multiple transformations at once, allowing you to, say, rotate an element and increase its size.

The CSS property in charge of transforms is called, unsurprisingly, the transform property. It needs to know the type of transformation you want and a value indicating how much to transform the element. For example, to rotate an element, you would use the keyword rotate, followed by the number of degrees to rotate it.

It's surprisingly easy to set up transforms. Listing 9-1 shows one in action.

Listing 9-1. A Basic Transform

```
<!DOCTYPE html>
<html>
<head>
    <title>Basic Transform</title>
    <style>

        #square {
            width: 150px;
            height: 150px;
            margin:4em;
            border: solid 3px green;
            background-color: red;
        }

        #square:hover {
            transform: scale(1.3) rotate(20deg);
        }

    </style>
</head>
<body>
<div id="square"></div>
</body>
</html>
```

Here we have a single div element with an id of square. In the CSS, we give it some basic styling, so that we can see it as a red square with a green border when we load it into a browser. The part in which we are interested is the transform property that we used within #square:hover. Here, we add two effects at once: a scale and a rotate effect. The scale function is given a number, a multiplication factor of 1.3, which causes it to scale up slightly larger than it initially appeared. The rotate is given a number suffixed with the CSS unit deg, which causes it to rotate 20 degrees.

■ **Tip** Some CSS units, like deg, make intuitive sense. Others, like the em unit used on the margin rule in the previous CSS code listing, often do not. An em is equal to the current font size. What this means is that, for example, if the font size of the document is 12 pt., 1 em is equal to 12 pt. Unlike pixels, which are an absolute measure, ems are scalable. This means that 2 em would equal 24 pt., 0.5 em would equal 6 pt., and so forth. The em is becoming increasingly popular in web documents, due to this scalability and the mobile-device-friendly nature of this.

This effect is surprisingly easy to accomplish. Figure 9-2 shows what it looks like in a web browser. On the left is the starting state, and on the right is the transformed state.

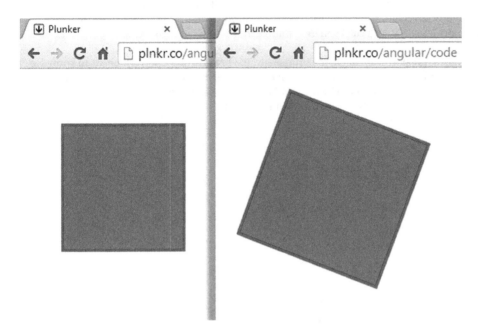

Figure 9-2. *A transform using* scale *and* rotate, *before and after*

This is all well and good, and transforms, in general, have many practical uses, but this is really just a two-frame animation. This is because the transform was applied as soon as the user hovered over the div element. One moment it was not rotated, then it was. Often, a more desirable effect can be achieved by getting the web browser to create a smooth transition from one state to the other. This is where CSS transitions come in.

One very important note about this and other code listings in this section is that I have omitted vendor prefixes. I have done this solely to avoid clutter and repetition, but the reality is that you will need to use them in your own projects. For example, the preceding transform property would generally look something like the following:

```
-webkit-transform: scale(1.3) rotate(20deg);
-moz-transform: scale(1.3) rotate(20deg);
-o-transform: scale(1.3) rotate(20deg);
-ms-transform: scale(1.3) rotate(20deg);
transform: scale(1.3) rotate(20deg);
```

Browser developers use CSS vendor prefixes to add new browser features that may not be part of a formal specification and to implement features in a browser specification that have not been finalized. This makes for a less than ideal situation in which you have to cover your bases so that the transform works across different browsers. If you are a fan of CSS preprocessors, such as SASS and Stylus, you will be used to vendor prefixes being handled for you automatically. If you aren't a fan of such tools, or if you have not discovered them yet, I recommend that you look into adopting one. These tools have a wide range of features that can make CSS much more intuitive and make you much more productive.

■ **Tip** You can learn more about SASS at `http://sass-lang.com/`. Stylus is a good alternative to SASS, and you can learn more about this one at `http://learnboost.github.io/stylus/`. There are other good CSS preprocessors out there; these just happen to be two I have personally used and found to be very effective and well-supported.

Transitions

Transforms can be fun in their own right, but they become even more interesting when coupled with CSS3 transitions. A transition is simply an animation from one set of CSS properties to another set of CSS properties, set to occur over a specified period of time. A transition has four key responsibilities: it must control which properties to animate; the duration of the animation, the type of animation, and (optionally) how long to wait before starting the animation.

A transition isn't an island unto itself; we need a few things in place before we can produce one. They are as follows:

- *Two styles*: One style is to represent the initial look of the element and another the end state of the transition, for example, an element that starts off at normal size but transitions to become two times larger.

- *The transition property*: This is the special ingredient that makes the animation possible. In general, you apply the transition property to the initial style of the element, the style that dictates the look of the element prior to the animation starting.

- *A trigger*: The trigger is the action that causes the transition between the two styles. Within CSS, you can use several pseudo-classes to trigger an animation: hover, active, focus, and so forth. You can also use JavaScript to trigger animations. Keep in mind that you only need to set a transition on an element once. The browser will take care of animating from one style to another and back to the original style, when the trigger no longer applies.

Look at Listing 9-2. This is a very basic example, but it shows each of the preceding points in practice.

Listing 9-2. Transitions in Action

```
<!DOCTYPE html>
<html>
<head>
    <title>A basic Transition</title>
    <style>
        .navButton {
            width: 100px;
            text-align: center;
            padding: .3em;
            background-color: orange;
            color: #000000;
            /* Transition width, color and background-color
                over half a second. */
            transition: width .5s, color .5s, background-color .5s
        }
```

```
        .navButton:hover {
            width: 110px;
            background-color: green;
            color: #ffffff;
        }
    </style>
</head>
<body>
<div class="navButton"> Home </div>
<div class="navButton"> About Us </div>
<div class="navButton"> Contact Us </div>
</body>
</html>
```

As you can see, we have two classes: the first one sets up the transition, and the second one is the end state of that transition. We have also explicitly stated which properties are to be transitioned and how long it should take for the transitions to complete. We have set a value of .5s (half a second) for each transition duration, though it is actually possible to give each CSS property a separate duration value (which can make for some very interesting effects).

The transition is triggered by users when they hover over one of the .navButton elements. You can use other pseudo-classes as triggers for animations too, such as transitioning a form field to a new color when the user tabs or clicks into it (using the :focus pseudo-class). You aren't limited to using pseudo-classes; you can create triggers yourself, using JavaScript to add and remove classes programmatically.

I can't show a screenshot of an animation, of course, but Figure 9-3 illustrates the start and end states. With the mouse over the About Us div, we can see that each of the properties we specified has indeed transitioned from one set of values to the other.

Figure 9-3. *Transitions*

Things can get really interesting when you combine transforms with transitions, so I will finish up with an example of how this is done. In fact, you already know how to do it, because transform is a property just like any other; therefore, it can be transitioned. Examine Listing 9-3.

Listing 9-3. Combining Transform and Transition

```
<!DOCTYPE html>
<html>
<head>
    <title>Transform and Transition</title>
    <style>

        .navButton {
            width: 100px;
            text-align: center;
```

```
            padding: .3em;
            background-color: orange;
            color: #000000;
            transition: all .5s;
        }

        .navButton:hover {
            width: 110px;
            background-color: green;
            color: #ffffff;
            transform:rotate(-6deg);
        }
    </style>
</head>
<body>
<div class="navButton"> Home </div>
<div class="navButton"> About Us </div>
<div class="navButton"> Contact Us </div>
</body>
</html>
```

This is essentially the same as Listing 9-2, with the differences shown in bold. Note the more concise transition declaration here. We've stated that all properties can be transitioned, and each of them should take half a second. The main addition is the transform property we see in .navButton:hover. Here, we set an end state with a rotation of -6 degrees, and we assume the default (0 degrees) rotation that implicitly exists in the initial state. Figure 9-4 shows the start and end states.

Figure 9-4. *Transitions combined with a transform*

An unusual aspect of transforms is that they don't really care what is going on around them. That is to say, they will obscure other elements as opposed to pushing them out of the way. As Figure 9-4 demonstrates, the About Us div has obscured the bottom right and the top left of the divs it originally sat neatly between. This isn't a good or a bad thing; it's just something to be aware of when you are planning how your effect or animation should work.

There is a whole lot more to CSS3 animation than the small glimpse offered here, but this should be just enough to help you get started in applying animations within Angular. There is an abundance of tutorials available online, and several good books available on the topic. I found the title *Pro CSS3 Animation* by Dudley Storey (Apress, 2012) to be a particularly focused and useful resource.

Applying Animations

You don't work directly with the $animate service when applying animations in Angular. Instead, you use supported directives and a special naming convention when writing your CSS. Essentially, you interact with the $animate service through CSS hooks that allow Angular to trigger your animations at certain points in a directives life cycle. This will make a lot more sense as we progress through this section.

We'll jump right in with a code listing. Listing 9-4 shows a fairly easy and common type of animation: a typical fade-in effect. This one is used simply to fade in a small piece of content when the Toggle Content button is clicked.

Listing 9-4. A Basic Fade-in Animation, animate-one.html

```html
<!DOCTYPE html>
<html ng-app="app">
<head>
    <title>Applying animations</title>
    <script src="js/angular.min.js"></script>
    <script src="js/angular-animate.js"></script>
    <script>
        var app = angular.module('app', ['ngAnimate']);
        app.controller('homeController', function ($scope) {
            $scope.on = false;
        });
    </script>
    <style>
        /* starting */
        .my-first-animation.ng-enter {
            transition: .5s all;
            opacity: 0;
        }

        /* ending */
        .my-first-animation.ng-enter.ng-enter-active {
            opacity: 1;
        }
    </style>

</head>
<body ng-controller="homeController">

<button ng-click="on=!on">Toggle Content</button>
<div class="my-first-animation" ng-if="on">
    This content will fade in over half a second.
</div>
</body>
</html>
```

There are a couple of very important things to note in Listing 9-4. We use a script reference to make sure that we pull in the ngAnimate module, and we declare a dependency on this module when we create our application module. These steps appear in bold, and they are the first steps I would recommend that you check whenever you run into any issues getting an animation to work.

The controller doesn't do very much at all, aside from setting a simple Boolean variable named on. We will get to its purpose shortly. It's interesting that there isn't more going on in the controller, given that we are performing an animation, but that's mainly because of the CSS-based approach to interacting with the ngAnimate service. Let's take a look at that now.

We have two CSS classes: one sets up the start of the animation, including the transition we want to use, and the second is the end state of the animation. We know that this is a fade-in effect, because we can see that the opacity starts out at 0 and finishes at 1 and that the transitions is dictating that this should occur over half a second. At this stage, we have set up the classes needed to perform the animation, but what we haven't done is tell Angular how and when it should use these classes. What we need is some way to hook this into the $animate service. This is where the naming conventions I mentioned earlier come into play.

The two CSS classes that we set up are used by Angular, but how and where did we tell Angular to use them? Many Angular directives support and trigger animations whenever any major event occurs during their life cycle. So, the trick to using the $animate service is to know which directives support animation and how to hook your CSS into that directive. Table 9-1 shows which animation events are triggered and what directive triggers them.

Table 9-1. *Supported Directives and Their Related Animation Events*

Directive	Animations
ngRepeat	enter, leave, and move
ngView	enter and leave
ngInclude	enter and leave
ngSwitch	enter and leave
ngIf	enter and leave
ngClass	add and remove
ngShow & ngHide	add and remove (the ngHide class value)

We are using the ngIf directive in our example, and we can see from Table 9-1 that the enter and leave events are supported. The way we hooked into these events was by setting the my-first-animation class on the directive, which I have shown again following:

```
<div class="my-first-animation" ng-if="on">
    This content will fade in over half a second.
</div>
```

This class name can be whatever you like, though you should take extra care to make sure that it won't clash with anything else in your code or any other libraries that you might happen to be using. This class is effectively the gateway into the $animate service, and it becomes the base class upon which we attach the Angular-generated classes. The enter event uses the class names ng-enter and ng-enter-active. Thus, in order to respond to these events through our own CSS, we made sure to add them to our base, or hook, class. Following, I've shown the class names again. These conform to the naming convention required, so that Angular can make use of them at the right moments in the directives life cycle.

```
.my-first-animation.ng-enter
.my-first-animation.ng-enter.ng-enter-active
```

As demonstrated in our example, these classes correspond to the start and end states of our animation. Keep in mind that we have combined both CSS classes for the end state class. This is simply to avoid any CSS specificity conflicts.

■ **Note** The supported directives will only make use of these classes if the `ngAnimate` module is present and you have set up the associated dependency, as discussed earlier in this section.

These classes only become active when Angular or more specifically in this case, the `ngIf` directive, determines that they are applicable. Of course, our ability to use this system relies on our knowing when these events take place. With that in mind, look at Table 9-2.

Table 9-2. *When Events Occur*

Event	Description
enter	When the new content is to be animated in
leave	When the former content is to be animated out
move	When a DOM element is moved from one position in the repeat list to another position
add	When the new CSS class is to be animated in
remove	When the old CSS class is to be animated out

Let's examine a slightly more involved animation example. This time, we will create a slider effect, sliding some content into view while sliding any existing content out of view. I hope that this will round off everything we have discussed so far and leave you fully prepared to tackle some serious experimentation. Ultimately, this will be the best way to come to grips with how the animation module works.

When you are reading through Listing 9-5, keep in mind that this time, we are animating for both the `enter` and the `leave` events, new content arriving (entering) and the original content leaving.

Listing 9-5. Sliding Content Animation, `animate-two.html`.

```
<!DOCTYPE html>
<html ng-app="app">
<head>
    <title>Applying animations</title>
    <script src="js/angular.min.js"></script>
    <script src="js/angular-animate.js"></script>
    <script>
        var app = angular.module('app', [ 'ngAnimate']);
        app.controller('homeController', ['$scope', function ($scope) {
            $scope.templates =
                    [
                        { name: 'Catie Grant', url: 'catie-grant.html'},
                        { name: 'Tara Court', url: 'tara-court.html'}
                    ];
            $scope.template = $scope.templates[0];
        }]);
    </script>

</head>
```

```
<body>
<div ng-controller="homeController">
    <select ng-model="template" ng-options="t.name for t in templates">
        <option value=""> none</option>
    </select>

    <div class="my-slide-animation-container">
        <div class="my-slide-animation" ng-include="template.url"></div>
    </div>
</div>
</body>
</html>
```

Through the ngInclude directive, Listing 9-5 also makes use of two included content files, which are shown in Listing 9-6 and Listing 9-7.

Listing 9-6. First Set of Content, catie-grant.html

```
<div>
    <h2>Catie Grant</h2>
    <p>Catie joined the company in 1998. She enjoys netball and hanging out with Tara.</p>
</div>
```

Listing 9-7. Second Set of Content, tara-court.html.

```
<div>
    <h2>Tara Court</h2>
    <p>Tara joined the company in 2004. She enjoys basketball and hanging out with Catie.</p>
</div>
```

Last, but by no means least, the CSS file that contains the animation classes is shown in Listing 9-8.

Listing 9-8. The CSS Animation Code

```
.my-slide-animation-container {
    position: relative;
    border: 1px solid black;
    height: 120px;
    overflow: hidden;
}

.my-slide-animation {
    padding-left: 5px;
}

/* set up the transition and position rules for enter and leave events */
.my-slide-animation.ng-enter, .my-slide-animation.ng-leave {
    transition: all ease-in 0.5s;
    position: absolute;
    top: 0;
    left: 0;
    right: 0;
    bottom: 0;
}
```

```
/* enter event - start class */
.my-slide-animation.ng-enter {
    top: -50px;
}

/* enter event - end class, leave event - start class */
.my-slide-animation.ng-enter.ng-enter-active, .my-slide-animation.ng-leave {
    top: 0;
}


/* leave event - end class */
.my-slide-animation.ng-leave.ng-leave-active {
    top: 100px;
}
```

Looking at the CSS in Listing 9-8, you can see that much of this is fairly standard, so I will only cover the bits that are relevant to our animation effect. It's difficult to tell much from a screenshot, though Figure 9-5 shows the initial state of play.

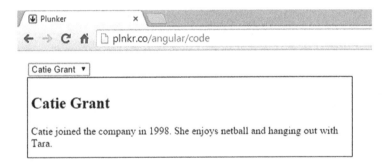

Figure 9-5. *The content slider*

Here's how it works: using the drop-down list, you can select a person. Once selected, the current person content will slide down and out of view, and the content for the currently selected person will slide up into view.

Crucial to understanding the CSS is the idea that we are creating hooks for both the enter and the leave events. Also, unlike our first example, we now have two animations running concurrently: the content being moved away and the content being moved in. The comments in the CSS explain the purpose of each class, and you can see that the start and end classes for both events all deal with the position of the content. It's either positioning it so that it is visible or positioning it so that it is hidden. Of course, the reason it doesn't just abruptly appear is because of the transition that we have set up on both my-slide-animation.ng-enter and my-slide-animation.ng-leave.

Let's turn our attention to Listing 9-5. You can see that we have taken care of the fundamental need to set up the ngAnimate dependency on our application module. As for the controller, all we do here is set up an array of objects, each of which is simply the name of a person and the location of a HTML file that contains content about that person (Listings 9-6 and 9-7 show the content of these two files). We put this array into the current scope via the templates property. Also, note that we set a default template in the current scope, so that the view doesn't start out empty.

There are a couple of interesting things going on in the view portion of this code listing. We can see an HTML select list that includes all of the template objects in the templates array and, importantly, which particular array item is bound to the template variable. This acts as the trigger that causes the animation to start.

This next line is the one that ties it all together. Note that the ngInclude directive uses the expression template.url. This will evaluate to the currently selected templates URL property.

```
<div class="my-slide-animation" ng-include="template.url"></div>
```

Let's not forget the all-important step of hooking our CSS into the ngInclude directive, by setting the class name.

If you have re-created these files in your AngularJS folder, you should be able to open them and see the animations in action. Remember, I haven't used vendor prefixes here, so you may have to add them, if you are using a browser that requires them. As I mentioned, if you are deploying any CSS animations in your own projects, you should be using the vendor prefixes. (I was using Chrome Version 37.0.2062.124 to run them as is.)

Summary

In this chapter, we studied how the ngAnimate module works. We saw that it is slightly unusual in that we do not directly interact with the $animate service, but we also saw that the hook system is quite easy to use, and it allows us the freedom to power our animations using CSS.

Hands-on experimentation is the key to learning most new languages, frameworks, and libraries, but I've found that this applies doubly in the case of learning to animate in Angular. It isn't difficult, but there are a few moving parts that are well worth exploring and tinkering with.

We only scratched the surface of what's possible with Angular animation, but it's quite likely that you won't need to dig too much deeper in order to do some productive work, particularly if you are already fairly handy with CSS and know your way around CSS3 animation. In most cases, you don't really want to get animation crazy. Usually, all you want to do is subtly draw the user's attention to the fact that something has changed.

CHAPTER 10

Deployment Considerations

Application deployment is an increasingly complex and multi-faceted topic. There is no quick answer as to how to approach it, because every application is unique. However, there are a number of best practices, techniques, and tools available that you should consider integrating into your workflow and build process. While the title of this chapter is Deployment Considerations, much of what is covered is applicable at the outset of a project right through to deployment and beyond.

In this chapter, we will take a brief look at some topics that are very likely to make their way onto your developer radar, once you have been using Angular for a while; topics that we don't really have time or space to cover in much detail in this book, but nonetheless they deserve a mention. You won't find much in-depth coverage here, as my aim is merely to introduce you to a sampling of the activities and issues that Angular developers often factor into their projects and workflows.

Configuration

We often want our Angular apps to run with different settings or configurations. For example, many web applications need to connect to a service of some kind so that they can interact with data sourced from the back-end. It is quite common to use one URL for the development server and another URL for the production server. In a scenario like this, we need to find a way to provide for configuration within our applications. Quite possibly the easiest way to use configuration within Angular is to set a constant with an object, which is the approach we will look at next.

It isn't uncommon for developers to create a separate module specifically for configuration. The code in Listing 10-1 below lives in a file named app.config.js.

Listing 10-1. app.config.js: setting up a constant

```
angular.module('app.config',[])
    .constant('myConfig', {
        'apiUrl': 'http://localhost:8080',
        'adminEmail': 'admin@mycompany.com'
    });
```

This module doesn't do much more than set up a constant called myConfig, as declared through the constant() methods first argument. The key point to observe here is that the second argument to the constant method is an object containing our configuration data; this object has two properties. We have one property containing the URL that our app should be using to communicate with the back-end and another property containing an email address the app can use to determine to whom to send support email.

This module isn't going to be of much use to anyone unless it can be accessed. As it is declared in a separate file, a script reference is needed. Also, we need to declare it as a dependency just as we would with any Angular module.

```
var app = angular.module('app', ['ngRoute', 'ngAnimate', 'app.config']);
```

Now it is just a matter of being able to access the myConfig constant so that we can access the configuration properties that it contains. Listing 10-2 shows an example of just that.

Listing 10-2. Using the configuration data in the app.config module

```
module.factory('memberDataStoreService', function ($http, myConfig) {

    var memberDataStore = {};

    memberDataStore.doRegistration = function (theData) {
        var promise = $http({method: 'POST', url: myConfig.apiUrl, data: theData});
        return promise;
    }

    return  memberDataStore;

})
```

Rather than hard code the value for the API URL, you can see here that we instead use the myConfig.apiUrl. There are other, more sophisticated approaches to managing application configuration; your specific needs may vary based on the kind of project on which you are working. We will look at a relatively common approach next.

A typical requirement is to have a set of configuration data for development and another set for production. Let's suppose that we have a locally installed database server with which our locally run development code communicates. Of course, once our code is deployed to our production server, we then want it to communicate with our production database. In this scenario, we have two sets of valid configuration data with which we could supply our app.

One way that we could handle this is to have two separate configuration modules—one for development and one for production. Listing 10-3 shows a module that we can use during development.

Listing 10-3. app.development.config..js: our development configuration

```
angular.module('app.development.config',[])
    .constant('myConfig', {
        'database-host': '127.0.0.1',
        'database-name: 'local-database'
});
```

You will notice that the myConfig object contains values specific to our locally installed database server. Pay particular attention to the fact that the module is named app.development.config. Listing 10-4 shows its counterpart: the production configuration module.

Listing 10-4. app.production.config.js: our development configuration

```
angular.module('app.production.config',[])
    .constant('myConfig', {
        'database-host': '168.63.165.103',
        'database-name: 'production-database'
});
```

This time we named the module `app.production.config`, and this time it contains production specific-configuration data. All that we need to do now is to tell our app which set of configuration data, or which module, we want it it to use. This can be achieved with a single change, as shown in the following example.

```
var app = angular.module('app', ['ngRoute', 'ngAnimate', 'app.development.config']);
```

In this particular case, we have provided our app with the development configuration data by specifying `app.development.config` as a dependency. The code that we are deploying to the production server would use `app.production.config`.

Testing

Testing is a huge topic in modern software development, and one that we have not touched on very much in this book. We barely have the time to do the topic justice, but I believe it is well worth singling out because Angular is designed with testability in mind, and testing is so very important.

There are several schools of thought about how and when to test—all valid and all with their own pros and cons. At a very high level the choices are generally one of the following:

- *Behavior-Driven Development (BDD)*: This approach dictates that we should write our tests first. In this scenario, we write tests to match the functionality that we will produce in the future.

- *Write-Behind Testing (WBT)*: This approach leaves testing until last, where we confirm the functionality works as expected after we have produced the code that is responsible for it.

- Writing tests to black-box test the functionality of the overall system.

Two extremely popular approaches these days are Behavior-Driven Development (BDD) and its cousin Test-Driven Development (TDD). Both are conceptually similar in that unit tests are written first and application code is produced later that will, once correct, pass these tests. This approach requires discipline and learning at least one unit-testing framework. A good unit-testing framework will make it easier to write and run your tests.

■ **Note**   The main differences between TDD and BDD are subtle but significant, owing to variations in the underlying mindset of the developer. Many consider BDD to be an improved version of TDD. I don't think one is necessarily better than the other, and both are valid options.

For the purposes of getting a general sense of what unit testing and Behavior-Driven Development is all about, we will consider a simple set of tests that revolve around some identified requirements for a typical login process. We will use Jasmine, a behavior-driven development framework for testing JavaScript code. Keep in mind, in this scenario, we have not yet written any application code; we are instead going to write an initial set of unit tests that we know we will need to run once we have produced the logic. In fact, in Listing 10-5, the Jasmine tests start out empty too.

Listing 10-5. An initial look at a set of tests

```
describe('user login form', function() {
    it('ensures invalid email addresses are caught', function() {});
    it('ensures valid email addresses pass validation', function() {});
    it('ensures submitting form changes path', function() { });

});
```

Starting off by writing a set of unit tests like this is a great way to get you thinking about what aspects of the code will need to be tested. It's perfectly fine just to start writing these out as the project requirements and use cases for a feature start to evolve.

This particular framework, called Jasmine, uses a describe function that itself contains several it functions. The describe function describes, through its first parameter, the purpose of the tests contained within; it's really just a title describing this particular set of unit tests. As these tests all pertain to the user login form, we named it user login form. Its second parameter is a function, and it is this function that contains the individual unit tests; the it() methods.

The it() methods' first parameter explains its purpose; this needs to be clear and descriptive. Its second parameter is a function; that is, the test itself. So that we can get a basic sense of what a test looks like, I will add some code to the "ensures valid email addresses pass validation test," which is the test described in the second it() method in Listing 10-6.

Listing 10-6. The "ensures valid email addresses pass validation test"

```
it('ensures valid email addresses pass validation', function() {
  var validEmails = [
        'test@test.com',
        'test@test.co.uk',
        'test734ltylytkliytkryety9ef@jb-fe.com'
     ];

for (var i in validEmails) {
        var valid = LoginService.isValidEmail(validEmails[i]);
        expect(valid).toBeTruthy();
     }

});
```

The test in Listing 10-6, as you can tell by its name, ensures valid email addresses pass validation. The most important statement is the one that has been set in bold. Here we use the expect() method to set up an expectation. This is chained to the toBeTruthy() matcher method. This statement will bring about the success or failure of the test. Should any of the email addresses in the validEmails array be invalid, this test will fail; otherwise, it will pass.

This pattern of having an expectation that is chained to a matcher is a very intuitive way to assert whether or not any given test should be deemed a success or a failure. A few examples, shown in Listing 10-7, should show the general pattern and a few of the expectations and matchers that come with the Jasmine unit test framework.

Listing 10-7. Sample expectations and matchers

```
// We expect 1 + 1 to equal 2.
// If it doesn't the test fails
expect(1 + 1).toEqual(2);

// We expect myObject to be null.
// If its not the test fails
var myObject = null;
expect(myObject).toBe(null);

// We expect null to be null
// If its not the test fails
expect(null).toBeNull();
```

```
// We expect the kids array to contain the string "Natalie"
// If it doesn't the test fails
var kids = ["Jenna", "Christopher", "Natalie", "Andrew", "Catie"];
expect(kids).toContain("Natalie");

// We expect 10 to be less than 15.
// If it isn't the test fails
expect(10).toBeLessThan(15);
```

Here we have five expectations, each with a corresponding matcher. Hopefully, you can see how expressive this is. It's not as difficult as you might think either; it doesn't take much work to write a test that will pass if, and only if, one plus one equals two. It was also quite easy to fail a test if a specific value is missing from an array. That being said, there is a lot more to know about unit testing and, even when you know it, doing it right can be quite an art form.

While we don't get chance to dive into testing fully in this book, I strongly encourage you to consider exploring the topic further. For me, writing tests with a good testing framework, and writing them up front, is a great way to get a sense that my application is watertight. When I change my application, I can run my tests again and make sure that it is still in good shape (and fix it if it isn't).

While I have focused on unit testing in this section, there are, of course, many other kinds of testing that you should consider conducting. Black box or end-to-end testing has its place, as does Write Behind Testing. I encourage you to make the time to dig deeper. Believe it or not, testing can actually be quite enjoyable and rewarding.

■ **Tip**   To find out more about Jasmine, you can visit `http://jasmine.pivotallabs.com/`. Other unit test frameworks include, but are certainly not limited to, qUnit (`http://qunitjs.com/`) and mocha (`http://visionmedia.github.io/mocha/`). Personally, I find it hard to pick a favorite from these, as they are all exceptionally good.

Error Handling

It can be tricky for developers who are new to JavaScript frameworks to figure out the best way to perform error handling; far too often we see applications that really don't have any strategy at all for doing so. As with most other topics in this chapter, we don't really get to dive into a lot of detail, but a few pointers will hopefully prompt you to consider developing some sort of error handling strategy. Fortunately, error handling is mostly about common sense and discipline.

First and foremost, you must have some kind of strategy in place. While it might be okay for debugging purposes, it really isn't okay to deploy your application with code such as that shown in Listing 10-8.

Listing 10-8. Lazy error handling

```
if(user.paySuccess()){
    // The users payment was succesful
    goToSuccessScreen();
}
else{
    // The users payment failed, pop up an alert
    // and log to the console.
    alert('An error has occured');
    console.log('An error has occured');
}
```

One problem here is that we inform the user about the error, but we don't actually help them to do anything about it. Another problem is that there is no communication back to us (or our support team) that this error occurred. We can do a little bit better. As there is little to gain by logging to the browsers console as we do in Listing 10-9, let's create a function for logging errors to the server instead.

Listing 10-9. A basic server logging mechanism

```
function log(sev, msg) {

    var img = new Image();
    img.src = "log.php?sev=" +
        encodeURIComponent(sev) +
        "&msg=" + encodeURIComponent(msg);
}
```

In Listing 10-9, we have a basic function that allows us to capture errors as they occur. This approach works by making an http GET request for an image on our web server. The image itself won't be visible within your application; it exists only as a way to pass the error information from the user's browser to our applications back-end. Listing 10-10 shows this in action.

Listing 10-10. Using a logging service

```
var paymentService = null;
try
{
    paymentService.payForItem();

}
catch(e){
    // alert user to the error
    showSomeFriendlyFeedback();
    // Trasmit the error to the server
    log(1, "001: The user was unable to complete his purchase");
}
```

There are a few noteworthy things happening in Listing 10-10. We are now using JavaScript's try/catch error handling construct; this is a much more elegant and readable approach than the one we took in Listing 10-6. For dramatic effect, we deliberately create an error within the try block by using the payForItem() method on an object that is null; this forces program execution into the catch block.

Now that we are within the catch block, we can discuss the two arguments that we provided to our log() method. The first argument is a severity level; in this case, we set the severity to 1, which is deemed to be the highest level of urgency. The next argument is a string that represents a description of the error. It is not uncommon to see error messages with numeric prefixes such as the "001" we use here. These can be quoted to support staff over the telephone and used to look for problem resolutions more effectively. They can also be used to locate information programmatically in a knowledge management system, for example.

With the nuts of bolts in place to do the logging, the next thing to consider is what to log and when to log it. Every application is different, but it goes without saying that anything you consider to be a severity level 1 should almost certainly be logged. Less severe or purely information logging should perhaps not be done at all. The last thing you want in very high traffic website is pointless logging requests that will only serve to place more strain on back-end systems rather than to provide help to developers or end users.

This is by no means the only way to do error handling, and you might want to consider an approach that will work well for your particular project. In some scenarios, it might well be better to log to the end user's device, though this is simply food for thought. I think it is fair to say that any approach at all is always better than the all-too-common no plan whatsoever.

■ **Caution** If you do choose to log information to the user's device, you need to consider the fact that this comes with some risk. The information is potentially accessible to other users, unless you put safeguards in place.

Hide Unprocessed Templates

Your Angular application needs to download your application scripts and the Angular scripts before it can go about its work. As you know, one aspect of this work is template processing; a job that can be done only once all of the required files are fully downloaded to the user's device. It is possible, particularly if your files are taking some time to download, that your end users will see the Angular interpolation expressions in their raw unprocessed form, as shown in Figure 10-1. This rather ugly looking, and potentially confusing, eyesore may only last for a split second or so, but it might well be something that you want to avoid,

Figure 10-1. *Unprocessed templates are an eyesore!*

The ng-cloak directive lets you hide (through the use of display: none) parts of the DOM tree until Angular is ready to process the whole page and make it live. You can hide a specific portion of the DOM tree, as we do in Listing 10-11.

Listing 10-11. Hiding a specific portion of the DOM tree

```
<h1 ng-cloak>Hello, {{name}}!</h1>
<p ng-cloak>It's great to see you again, you haven't logged in since {{lastLoggedIn}}</p>
```

Alternatively, you can hide the entire page by using ng-cloak at a higher level in the DOM tree. In Listing 10-12 we apply ng-cloak on the controller element itself, thereby hiding everything in one fell swoop.

Listing 10-12. Hiding a larger portion of the DOM tree

```
<div ng-controller="HelloCtrl" ng-cloak>
   <h1>Hello, {{name}}!</h1>
   <p>It's great to see you again, you haven't logged in since {{lastLoggedIn}}</p>
   <p>We hope you have a {{typeOfDay}} day!</p>
</div>
```

The approach you take is likely to depend on the way your application is structured. That is, if the first screen of your application consists of parts which are mostly dynamic, you might want to hide the whole page by placing the ng-cloak directive on the controller element, or even the <body> tag. Otherwise, you might want to use the ng-cloak directive on an element-by-element basis, so that users can view the static portions of the page while your application scripts finish loading and are ready to bootstrap the application.

Essentially, ng-cloak is simply a way of temporarily applying the CSS code display: none; to the element upon which it is declared. However, it is not the only solution to this problem. Another option that you might want to consider is to not use the double curly braces at all. Instead, you can use the ng-bind directive.

Listing 10-13. The ngBind directive in action

```
<div ng-controller="HelloCtrl">
    Hello, <span ng-bind="name"></span>!
</div>
```

If you adopt the approach shown in Listing 10-13, you will not see anything other than empty space in the case of lengthy script downloads. An empty span tag will appear momentarily. Perhaps this is a better approach than an unpleasant looking unprocessed expression?

Minification and Bundling

Many Angular apps are made up of a number of potentially large files; each of which must be requested by the user's web browser and then transmitted across the network. A two-fold concern here could be how to trim the files down to much smaller sizes and how to keep the number of network requests for such files to a minimum. A process known as *minification* and *bundling* is typically applied in these situations.

Think about how well formatted your JavaScript source code is; it is (hopefully) well commented and has lots of spaces and tabs that help to make easy to read. This is great from the point of view of a developer, as it makes life simpler. At the end of the day though, the JavaScript interpreter doesn't care about any of this. Consider the two code listings that follow. You don't need to understand the code, just consider the fact that Listing 10-14 and Listing 10-15 are functionally identical.

Listing 10-14. Typical unminified source code

```
function getElementsByClassName(className) {
        var results = [];
        walkTheDOM(document.body, function (node) {
            var array,                  // array of class names
                ncn = node.className; // the node's classname

// If the node has a class name, then split it into a list of simple names.
// If any of them match the requested name, then append the node to the list of results.
```

```
        if (ncn && ncn.split(' ').indexOf(className) >= 0) {
                        results.push(node);
        }
    });
    return results;
}
```

Listing 10-14 is the original source code. Listing 10-15 is a minified version of the same source code. It's not pretty is it? However, it produces a much smaller file, and it will require far less time to make it from the server to the user's browser. Sure, the comments are gone, the spaces and tabs are gone, and even the variable names have been changed to something less recognizable, but the JavaScript interpreter doesn't care about any of this, and the end result is exactly the same.

Listing 10-15. Minified source code

```
function getElementsByClassName(e){var t=[];walkTheDOM(document.body,function(n)
{var r,i=n.className;if(i&&i.split(" ").indexOf(e)>=0){t.push(n)}});return t}
```

If your source code files are large, minification can make a significant difference to the perceived performance and actual load times of your applications. Converting source code files to minified versions is not complicated either, because there are plenty of tools and websites that can do this conversion for you. A particularly good way to handle this is by using UglifyJS (https://github.com/mishoo/UglifyJS2); which calls itself a JavaScript parser, minifier, compressor, or beautifier toolkit.

Bundling is slightly different but often goes hand-in-hand with minification. The idea behind *bundling* is that you take a number of files and merge them all into just one file. For example, you might be using several Angular files (the standard angular JavaScript file and, say, two more JavaScript files for routing and animation) and your own applications files. As you would expect, each of these files causes a separate network request. Consolidating all of these files into just one file means that there will be just one network request for the consolidated file; this can lead to a decent performance boost. As with minification, you don't need to do this yourself, as there are many tools available that will do it for you.

If you decide to use these techniques, be sure to test your application in its minified and bundled form. Minifying, in particular, can be problematic due to the way that Angular uses dependency injection; so it's usually just a case of finding an approach that is Angular friendly. You might consider looking at ng-annotate, which at the time of writing, can be found at https://github.com/olov/ng-annotate.

Managing the Build Process

From a front-end perspective, it seems like only yesterday that websites and applications were nowhere near complex enough to need dedicated build tools and task runners. Those days are gone; today they are rich in features and functionality. This additional complexity has brought about the rise of tools such as Grunt and Gulp, both of which are often termed task runners or build tools.

As I have hinted at throughout this chapter, there are often a number of things that you might need to consider before you deploy your website to a production server. You might need to minify and bundle your application source files, you might want to run a set of tests to make sure that your application is still watertight and free of bugs, and you might want to adjust your configuration to reflect the live environment instead of the development or staging environment. That's a lot of work, and often there is much more to do.

Tools such as Grunt and Gulp can automate this work, and they have proven to be a huge advantage in both large and small applications alike.

To illustrate what a task runner does, let's take a quick look at Grunt. In the Grunt world, you create a JavaScript file called Gruntfile.js and then you configure and load your tasks using JavaScript. Listing 10-16 shows an example of what a Grunt.js file might look like.

Listing 10-16. A sample Gruntfile

```
module.exports = function (grunt) {

// Part One

    // Configure the various tasks we want to run

    grunt.initConfig({
        watch: {
            build: {
                files: 'src/**/*.*',
                tasks: ['uglify', 'copy'],
                options: {
                    livereload: true
                }
            }
        },
        uglify: {
            options: {
                mangle: true
            },
            my_target: {
                files: {
                    'site/js/js.min.js': ['src/js/*.js']
                }
            }
        },
        copy: {
            main: {
                files: [
                    // includes files within path and its sub-directories
                    {expand: true, cwd: 'src/', src: ['**', '!**/assets-master/**', '!**/css/**',
                    '!**/js/**'], dest: 'site/'}

                ]
            }
        }
    });

// Part Two

    // Load the tasks we have just configured
    grunt.loadNpmTasks('grunt-contrib-watch');
    grunt.loadNpmTasks('grunt-contrib-uglify');
    grunt.loadNpmTasks('grunt-contrib-copy');

    // The task we want to run by default when we start Grunt
    grunt.registerTask('default', ['watch']);

}
```

There is a lot going on in this file and, if you haven't used Grunt before, you will almost certainly need to follow a decent tutorial to get at the finer details. However, the main things to observe are that in the first part of the script (commented as Part One), a set of tasks is configured. In the second part (commented as Part Two), those tasks are loaded and made ready for use on the command line. Now, assuming we have Grunt installed, we can start Grunt and enter the grunt command. Grunt will then proceed to perform a number of tasks on our behalf. It will:

- Start to monitor files and directories for changes (the `grunt-contrib-watch` task).

- Minify and bundle our source code files when they change (the `grunt-contrib-uglify` task).

- Copy our source code files and any assets into a distribution folder ready for deployment (the `grunt-contrib-copy` task).

In this particular script, it is the `grunt-contrib-watch` task that is started when we launch Grunt, as we made it the default task. Should this task observe any changes within the configured directories, it will in turn run the `grunt-contrib-minify` and `grunt-contrib-copy` tasks. The end result is a batch of processed files that are placed in an output directory ready for us to deploy. Though not used here, there are even Grunt tasks that can handle that step for us too!

You could learn to use a task runner such as Grunt or Gulp in about half a day or so, perhaps even less. Tools like this really can change your workflow in amazing ways. If you find that you have reached a point where you are manually performing lots of tasks, you should seriously consider looking into adopting a task runner.

You can learn much more about Grunt at `http://gruntjs.com/`. Gulp takes a slightly different approach, but it is essentially the same kind of tool with a similar, perhaps lower, learning curve. You can find more information on Gulp at `http://gulpjs.com/`.

Deployment

Deployment is *all of the activities that make a software system available for use*. As with most of the other things we have touched upon in this chapter, the implementation details can vary wildly from project to project and organization to organization.

For many developers, gone are the days where a simple FTP connection to a remote server was all that was needed in order to transfer files from your local machine to a production environment. For small websites this is still a valid approach in some cases. However, because web development projects are becoming increasingly more complex, the teams that work on them need ways to manage this.

If you look at the diagram in Figure 10-2 you will see a typical FTP approach to deployment. FTP, or File Transfer Protocol, is a time tested and reliable means of moving files from one network location to another. The chances are high that have used FTP before or have some basic understanding of what it is used for. Here the developer has opened an FTP connection (using an FTP client such as FileZilla or cuteFTP) and used it to transfer code and assets from her machine to the remote server. At this point the website (or changes to an existing website) is available to the end users.

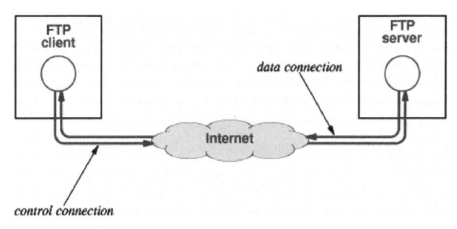

Figure 10-2. *Simple FTP approach to moving files to a web server*

This approach works well enough, but problems start to occur when projects become larger and more involved.

■ **Tip**   The File Transfer Protocol (FTP) is a standard network protocol used to transfer computer files from one host to another host over a TCP-based network, such as the Internet.

One added complexity in such cases is that multiple developers must be able to access and edit the source code, and they must be aware of what other developers and stakeholders are up to. Certain question must be asked and answered. How do we manage the source code? How do we test that it all works once changes have been made to it? How do we move successfully tested code into the production environment without stumbling upon configuration errors and other mistakes? How do we communicate the status of the project to other developers and stakeholders?

Such questions, and many others like them, are often addressed through a process known as Continuous Integration. This topic could, and does, fill entire books, so we will only scratch the surface here.

Continuous Integration, often referred to as CI, is essentially any system which allows a group of developers and other stakeholders to frequently and easily update, build, test and deploy changes to software. More often than not, much of this process is automated. A typical CI process would address at least the following objectives.

1. Maintain a code repository

2. Automate the build

3. Test the code

4. Report the status of the system

5. Automate deployment

As a developer you are very likely to encounter the need to maintain a code repository (objective 1) as this will require you to use a version control system of some form. For example, your team might have chosen to use GIT, a popular distributed version control system, to pull code files from a remote source code repository so that you can carry out tasks such as adding new features or fixing bugs. At some point later you would commit your changes and then push your work back to the version control system. Tools such as GIT help you to identify and resolve any conflicts that your changes (or the changes of other developers) may have introduced. They also make sure that your changes can be seen and accessed by other developers on your team.

■ **Tip**   Git is a very popular option for source control, though it can be confusing for beginners. You can find a great introductory, though very thorough, tutorial at `https://www.atlassian.com/git/tutorials/`.

One of the handy things about a good CI process is that it can be triggered when a developer places their changes back into the remote code repository. Have a look at Figure 10-3.

Figure 10-3.   *A high level look at Continous Integration*

At a very high level this diagram depicts a typical CI process. The developer has committed and pushed her code changes to the version control system; now her changes are available to the rest of the team. Of particular note here is that the act of pushing up these changes to the version control system has triggered a build of the code. The build can be a very complicated affair and the CI process is often tailored to manage this complexity on your behalf. Figure 10-3 shows that after the code is successfully built we run tests; this is a crucial part of the whole process as it will prevent broken software going into production. Another crucial aspect of the process is the reporting because developers and other stakeholders need to be aware of what has occurred (this is often available as a report in the CI system and sent to the team via email).

Why do we call this process Continuous Integration? Primarily because this whole cycle can be run many times a day (continuous) and it integrates many related aspects of the build and deployment process. Putting a sophisticated CI process in place is often a project in itself, but generally speaking, as a developer, your entry point into all this is through the version control system. While you may not be exposed to the complexities of setting up a CI process, it is useful to see the contrast between the simple FTP approach we discussed above and the much more involved CI process we just touched upon.

Summary

At the beginning of this chapter, I asserted that application deployment is an increasingly complex and multi-faceted topic. This is indeed true, but hopefully I have given you a sense that there are tools and techniques that you can use to manage this. While we didn't go into much detail, there are plenty of books and online resources that are dedicated to these topics. It can seem overwhelming, even for seasoned pros, but you don't have to use any of these techniques if you simply don't need them. The real trick is to keep your eye out for anything that can make your life simpler, and learn more about it as and when you need it.

This chapter brings us to the end of this book, but it is, of course, only the start of the Angular learning process. We had a brief look at JavaScript in the first chapter, and then we moved on to the more abstract topics of MVC and high level application design. We also looked at key Angular topics, such as directives, filters, and the routing system. Still, there is plenty more to learn and lots of fun to be had doing so. You will find no shortage of great Angular resources online, including the very useful Angular developer guide on the main Angular website at `https://docs.Angular.org/guide`, and my colleague Adam Freeman's amazingly in-depth *Pro Angular* book (Apress, 2014).

Index

Get the eBook for only $10!

Now you can take the weightless companion with you anywhere, anytime. Your purchase of this book entitles you to 3 electronic versions for only $10.

This Apress title will prove so indispensible that you'll want to carry it with you everywhere, which is why we are offering the eBook in 3 formats for only $10 if you have already purchased the print book.

Convenient and fully searchable, the PDF version enables you to easily find and copy code—or perform examples by quickly toggling between instructions and applications. The MOBI format is ideal for your Kindle, while the ePUB can be utilized on a variety of mobile devices.

Go to www.apress.com/promo/tendollars to purchase your companion eBook.